D1059361

of these complexities is absolutely amazing and gives single parents a road map to a life where they can *thrive*! This is a life-changing resource . . . a *must* read!"

—Tammy G. Daughtry, MMFT, founder, CoParenting International, and author of *Co-Parenting Works! Helping Your Children Thrive After Divorce*

"Powerful, personal, and uplifting! Parenting is the world's hardest job, and how much more is parenting alone. With years of experience supporting and guiding single parents, and drawing on personal experiences, Linda Jacobs offers simple, supportive, and spiritual advice for the parent searching for hope. Read, relate, and refer!"

—Dr. Jensen Petersen, First Baptist Church of Navarre, Florida

"Single parenting is hard work. There is no one who knows how to maneuver through these obstacles better than Linda Jacobs. In *The Single Parent*, Linda deals with the difficult subjects head on and applies biblical truths to our everyday situations. With over fifty years of hands-on experience, she challenges all single parents to be the best that we can be with practical tools and honest answers."

—Krista Smith, founder, Sonset Point Ministries, and author

"Single parents can thrive! Linda empowers parents with a biblical, practical approach that brings hope and encouragement to the soul. This is a must read for any single parent. I highly recommend this insightful work by someone who has been in the trenches."

—Dr. Scott Turansky, National Center for Biblical Parenting

"This book landed in my hands at the perfect time! Linda does a beautiful job of showing the single parent how God is with us in this season! She also gives amazing advice on some very common places we can get stuck on this journey! A must read for sure."

—Nicole Wallis, single mom

the single parent

the
singleparent

confident and successful

Linda Ranson Jacobs
Creator of the **DivorceCare for Kids** program

BETHANYHOUSE
a division of Baker Publishing Group
Minneapolis, Minnesota

Published by Bethany House Publishers
11400 Hampshire Avenue South
Bloomington, Minnesota 55438
www.bethanyhouse.com

Bethany House Publishers is a division of
Baker Publishing Group, Grand Rapids, Michigan

Printed in the United States of America

Library of Congress Cataloging-in-Publication Data
Names: Jacobs, Linda Ranson, author.
Title: The single parent : confident and successful / Linda Ranson Jacobs.
Description: Minneapolis : Bethany House, a division of Baker Publishing Group, 2019.
Identifiers: LCCN 2018053580| ISBN 9780764232848 (trade paper : alk. paper) | ISBN 9781493418657 (ebook)
Subjects: LCSH: Single mothers—Religious life. | Parenting—Religious aspects—Christianity. | Child rearing—Religious aspects—Christianity.
Classification: LCC BV4519.18 .J325 2019 | DDC 248.8/45—dc23
LC record available at https://lccn.loc.gov/2018053580

Unless otherwise indicated, Scripture quotations are from the HOLY BIBLE, NEW INTERNATIONAL VERSION®. Copyright © 1973, 1978, 1984 Biblica. Used by permission of Zondervan. All rights reserved.

Scripture quotations identified ESV are from The Holy Bible, English Standard Version® (ESV®), copyright © 2001 by Crossway, a publishing ministry of Good News Publishers. Used by permission. All rights reserved. ESV Text Edition: 2016

Scripture quotations identified KJV are from the King James Version of the Bible.

Scripture quotations identified NIV are from the Holy Bible, New International Version®. NIV®. Copyright © 1973, 1978, 1984, 2011 by Biblica, Inc.™ Used by permission of Zondervan. All rights reserved worldwide. www.zondervan.com. The "NIV" and "New International Version" are trademarks registered in the United States Patent and Trademark Office by Biblica, Inc.™

Scripture quotations identified NLT are from the Holy Bible, New Living Translation, copyright © 1996, 2004, 2007, 2013, 2015 by Tyndale House Foundation. Used by permission of Tyndale House Publishers, Inc., Carol Stream, Illinois 60188. All rights reserved.

Scripture quotations identified NRSV are from the New Revised Standard Version of the Bible, copyright © 1989 National Council of the Churches of Christ in the United States of America. Used by permission. All rights reserved.

Scripture quotations identified RSV are from the Revised Standard Version of the Bible, copyright 1946, 1952 [2nd edition, 1971] National Council of the Churches of Christ in the United States of America. Used by permission. All rights reserved worldwide.

Scripture quotations identified TLB are from The Living Bible, copyright © 1971. Used by permission of Tyndale House Publishers, Inc., Carol Stream, Illinois 60188. All rights reserved.

Cover design by Rob Williams, InsideOutCreativeArts

19 20 21 22 23 24 25   7 6 5 4 3 2 1

green press INITIATIVE

Contents

Introduction

Life Lessons Single Parents Can Learn from the Bible

She was . . . and then she wasn't.

She had funny, lovable, laughing kids . . . and then she didn't.

She could sponsor a child for church camp or a mission trip . . . and then she couldn't.

She would laugh and joke with her friends and co-workers . . . and then she wouldn't.

She fell into a deep, dark hole where there wasn't a way out . . . and then there was.

In the five statements above is my story, and if you are a single parent, in some ways it might be your story also. Whether you are a single dad or a single mom, you have a story. We all have different stories, and our stories need to be told.

They need to be told to encourage each other and to lift up one another. They need to be told so others won't make the same mistakes some of us made. Our stories need to be told now, while we remember them, so that later we can tell them to our children and our children's children. Your story could be just the hope someone needs to keep moving forward in his or her life.

Being a single parent isn't all about surviving. Oh, maybe the first few years of parenting alone might focus on survival, but as time goes on, wonderful and funny things happen. As long as a night can be, joy comes in the morning. "Weeping may linger for the night, but joy comes with the morning" (Psalm 30:5 NRSV).

My Story

Allow me to share a little more of my tale, so briefly sketched in the five lines above.

She was . . . and then she wasn't.

I was married and then I wasn't. It was a shock to my system. I had never believed in divorce—still don't—and yet I'm divorced. I was no longer a wife. I no longer had a mate. I was no longer a part of someone. God had pulled us together, and man separated us.

She had funny, lovable, laughing kids . . . and then she didn't.

My children were funny and lovable little kids. I really enjoyed their sense of humor and their personality quirks. It seemed like they were always laughing and kidding around. Then all of sudden they were not happy. They were sullen, angry, depressed, defiant, and worried.

She could sponsor a child for church camp or a mission trip . . . and then she couldn't.

When my children were preschool and early elementary age we sponsored a lot of teens by paying their deposits for church camp. Sometimes we paid the entire amount for church camp or for a mission trip. In other words, we had the funds to help others. And then I found myself barely able to feed my own children. I could no longer help others at church.

She would laugh and joke with her friends and co-workers . . . and then she wouldn't.

I owned two child care centers and loved my job. I enjoyed joking and laughing with my staff. I loved going to church and visiting my brothers and sisters in Christ. I was the first one to throw my head back and laugh uproariously at a joke. And then I didn't. I was in such turmoil and kept everything inside—it seemed as though the world around me no longer existed. Nothing was funny anymore. I wept late at night. I mumbled my way through my day at work.

She fell into a deep, dark hole where there wasn't a way out . . . and then there was.

I fell into such a pit that I felt I would never be able to claw my way out of it. I thought it was the end of my life—and it was the end of the life I had known for many years. I tried to pray, but my prayers seemed to reach only the ceiling of my bedroom. I tried to read God's Word, but the words just blurred on the page.

What I thought was a nightmare that would never end eventually did end. I won't bore you with all the details of my story, but I want you to know that through the Holy Spirit ministering to me, through Christian brothers and sisters mentoring me, and through God's Word, ever so slowly a new me and a new life emerged. There was a way out of the deep, dark hole after all.

What Happened to My Kids and to Me along the Way

My kids were seven and eleven years old when their dad left the first time. (He moved out more than once.) Those two kids grew up to be wonderful contributing adults in our society today. My daughter, Julie, has recently retired from the air force. While in the air force she received many accolades. She served our country well and with honor. My son worked his way through college and medical school and today is Dr. Brian Ranson, an anesthesiologist in Texas.

Both kids are married and have given me outstanding grandchildren. We survived. We laughed. We found joy in the midst of trials. We prayed together. We read God's Word together. We supported each other. The kids brought their friends home to talk to me when their friends couldn't talk to their own parents. We created family. (More later on how we accomplished these feats.)

Through my journey as a single parent, I found I had skills that I didn't know I possessed. Other than in a college speech class, I had never given a speech before my divorce. Now I speak at children's ministry conferences, at family ministry conferences, before schools, at retreats, and at blended family events. I even spoke before a legislative task force once and also at the National Technical Assistance Center for the Children's Mental Health Training Institute at Georgetown University. Why am I telling you these things? Not to brag, but to let you know that I stand in awe of what God has done. I am still amazed, all these years later, at what God did, is doing, and will do with my life.

I also didn't know that I could write, but through all those trials I learned I could. I've had articles published in *Children's Ministry*, *Focus on the Family*, and *KidzMatter* magazines, and I can't even remember where else.

I wrote and developed DC4K,[1] DivorceCare for Kids, a curriculum kit and program for children whose parents are separated or divorced. I also write a blog, *Kids & Divorce*,[2] which has over three hundred articles for church leaders and children's ministers. I've written an e-book[3] and print book,[4] both aimed at church leadership, and now this book, *The Single Parent: Confident and Successful*.

Allow me to encourage you. Don't limit yourself or put yourself in a box. Don't try to put God in a box either. He has plans for you. "For surely I know the plans I have for you, says the Lord, plans for your welfare and not for harm, to give you a future with hope" (Jeremiah 29:11 NRSV).

The Single Parent is not a book about how to survive a divorce or the death of a spouse. It's not about how one becomes a single parent. It is a book to help you learn how to be a better single parent and to encourage you through the Word of God.

Some stories in this book may hit you head on. You'll empathize and connect with the people in the stories. Other stories may not apply to your particular situation, but my prayer is that you'll remember them so God can use you to help another single parent. At the end of each chapter is a "Going Deeper" section, which you can use to help you invest in the Scriptures and to gain a better understanding of the issues presented. Or you can use the "Going Deeper" section in a small-group study.

Whether you are parenting alone due to a death, divorce, adoption, or some other situation, this book is designed to encourage you in your journey of parenting alone and to help you avert problems before they arise. Real-life stories are told in this book—my stories as well as those of the many single moms and dads who have come across my path through the years. While *The Single Parent* won't answer all of your questions, it will help you be creative in your parenting abilities.

When I became a single parent, I didn't know there were single parents in the Bible. I didn't realize there were Scriptures that would apply to me, that would grow me and help create a closer relationship with Father God. I thought that God had more or less deserted me after my divorce. But God was there all the time.

Is He there all the time for you? I hope you find out that He is through the stories and Scriptures in this book.

1

Loneliness: One of the Hardest Parts of Being a Single Parent

"God Sets the Lonely in Families"

She was . . . and then she wasn't!

Every time one of my kids had an event, I attended and I sat there alone. I would see men with their arms around their wives' shoulders. I watched as kids rushed from the stage after the concert toward their dads. The dads would ruffle their kids' hair, hug them fiercely, or pick their kids up and squeeze them with pride. The year before, when I had been married and my husband traveled, I went to these same events by myself, but I didn't feel alone. You see, I knew that when I got home my husband would call, and I would tell him all about the concert and the other events of the day. We would laugh as we talked about the kids.

The difference then was the fact that I had a two-parent family. Then we divorced, and I felt like I no longer had a family. It was just the kids and me. There was no one to share the day's events with and no one to talk with about the funny things the kids did or their accomplishments. I felt I was totally alone.

How many times have you looked around and felt that everyone must be married and part of a family except you? You see those families in the grocery store, at the ball games, at school events, and at church. As single parents, we have a tough road to travel, and then we go to church and hear Psalm 68:6, "God sets the lonely in families." Maybe you read this Scripture in your private Bible study time and stumbled over what it was supposed to mean to you.

When I read this I had to stop and say, "But, God, what about me? I'm lonely. I have children, and yet I don't feel like I have a family." Or what about the father who lives alone without his children and only gets to see them every other weekend? Does he think, *Well, God, what about me? I love my children, yet here I sit alone without them?* Or the widow: *God, what about me? I was in a family, and now my helpmate is no longer living. What about me? I am so lonely that every part of my being hurts. What about me, God?*

What Is God's Declaration Concerning Loneliness?

In Genesis 2:18 we find that "the Lord God said, 'It is not good for man to be alone. I will make a helper suitable for him.'"

God in His infinite wisdom could see and know that Adam was lonely. Even though God had created the most beautiful, perfect world and had taken care of all of Adam's physical needs and had surrounded him with every animal, fish in the sea, and fowl of the air, God knew that Adam needed someone like himself. God knows that we need people around us. He knows that sometimes we need someone with "skin on."

God is always with us; He is always there, cradling us in His arms. But how many times late at night have you just needed to talk with someone? It may have been a time when you were experiencing a problem with one of your children, or possibly you were just hurting or feeling lonely. A minister once told me that all I needed was God, that I didn't need anyone else. Evidently, this minister had never been a single parent, and one has to wonder if he had ever read Genesis 2:18.

Don't feel guilty when you want someone with whom you can sit and talk. God understands that as humans we need to have people around us.

"Adam's aloneness was not a mistake by a God who is sovereign and all-knowing. Instead, God's declaration is evidence that being created in the image of God includes being relational. God has designed us with an inherent need for intimacy with Him AND with other persons who are significant to us," write the authors of *Discovering Intimacy*.[1]

When I speak at retreats for single parents, I address the issue of loneliness head on. Following are some of the responses I have received after asking participants to "think about the following statement and then write out the scenario that comes to mind: *I remember a time when I was very lonely. It was when . . .*"

- My grandmother died, and I didn't have anyone to console me in my grief.
- I had a New Year's Eve party. My house was full of people, and everyone had someone—and I didn't.
- The youth group got together after church. All the parents were there, and I was shunned by the moms.
- I walked into the house after my husband died.
- I had just found out my son was diagnosed with autism. How on earth would I get through raising an autistic son by myself?
- My son was in track, and sitting at a track meet by myself was excruciating.
- My best friend was getting married, and she wanted me to be her bridesmaid. My husband had just died five months before. As I stood beside her I couldn't quit weeping. I was so happy for her but had never felt lonelier than at that moment.

- I attended school conferences. Every school conference after we divorced was when I felt my loneliest.
- At night I'm lying in bed, and it's dark and quiet.
- On Friday nights of my ex's weekend and the long weekend is stretched out before me; I feel so very lonely and missing my kids the minute they walk out the door.
- I was at church! Church was where I felt the loneliest.

What Is God's Decision Concerning Loneliness?

Even though we tend to think we are the first generation, nation, or century to face so many family problems, we are no different from people in biblical times, when families faced war, famine, slavery, isolation, and the splitting apart of family units. What happened in the Bible when families were torn apart or people found themselves alone and not part of a family?

In the Old Testament, we read about Naomi in the book of Ruth. Naomi, like many of us, did not start out being alone. She was married and had children, and then her husband died. Unlike women in today's world, Naomi had no way of supporting herself.

> In the days when the judges ruled, there was a famine in the land, and a man from Bethlehem in Judah, together with his wife and two sons, went to live for a while in the country of Moab. The man's name was Elimelech, his wife's name Naomi, and the names of his two sons were Mahlon and Kilion. They were Ephrathites from Bethlehem, Judah. And they went to Moab and lived there. Now Elimelech, Naomi's husband, died, and she was left with her two sons. They married Moabite women, one named Orpah and the other Ruth. After they had lived there about ten years, both Mahlon and Kilion also died, and Naomi was left without her two sons and her husband.
>
> Ruth 1:1–5

Do you think Naomi was lonely after the loss of her husband and sons? Like many of us, Naomi was left in a crisis mode. I imagine she was grieving and wondering, *How am I going to survive? I've lost my husband and my children. I am so alone.* As you read the book of Ruth, you learn that Naomi decided to return to Judah, and one of her daughters-in-law chose to go with her. The daughter-in-law, Ruth, eventually married and had a child. And Naomi was adopted into a family:

The women said to Naomi: "Praise be to the Lord, who this day has not left you without a kinsman-redeemer. May he become famous throughout Israel! He will renew your life and sustain you in your old age. For your daughter-in-law, who loves you and who is better to you than seven sons, has given him birth." Then Naomi took the child, laid him in her lap and cared for him. The women living there said, "Naomi has a son." And they named him Obed. He was the father of Jesse, the father of David.

Ruth 4:14–17

As you can see, these people created a different kind of family unit. They made a surrogate family.

Therapist Carmen Hoffman[2] writes in *Single Parent Magazine,*

We make surrogate families through friends, community or work contacts—especially when our biological families are insufficient or unavailable. As believers, we have a dual family membership through Christ's body, the church. We bond by sharing our lives, successes and failures. As with all families, commitment, struggle, laughter and shared experiences strengthen the emotional glue.

Jesus never endorsed a particular family form. Instead, He gave us examples of how the church constituted our primary family. In three gospels, Jesus declares that His brother and sisters do the will of the heavenly Father.

All through the Bible, people created surrogate families.

Jesus said in Luke 8:21, "My mother and brothers are those who hear God's word and put it into practice."

In Mark 3:34, we read that Jesus "looked at those seated in a circle around him and said, 'Here are my mother and my brothers! Whoever does God's will is my brother and sister and mother.'"

People need and want to belong. In today's society, the church can become the surrogate family. The church is and should be the family of God. A family meets each other's needs and cares for one another.

The Story of a Desperate Single Mom

Melissa, a single mom with two elementary school–age daughters, joined our church. I began to mentor and help Melissa survive her lonely single-parent journey. She was renting one bedroom for herself and two daughters from a local woman. Because she had only one room, she kept everything she didn't need at the moment in a storage unit. As people gave her items, such as a used washer and dryer, she put the items in the storage unit. She kept most of the kids' toys in the unit along with clothes and other seasonal items that weren't needed yet.

One day she went to switch out summer clothes for warmer clothes and noticed the lock had been cut. As she raised the door, she discovered an empty storage unit. Every single item was gone. There was nothing left—no clothes, no school backpacks, not even the boogie boards her little girls had used that summer. She called me immediately, in tears.

She was devastated. She was just about ready to give up. I contacted the people who had been in our Single & Parenting[3] group, and they all began praying for her and texting her encouraging messages.

When the mission team heard about her situation, they called and said, "We're having a church garage sale. Come and pick out some dishes and things you think that single mom will need."

We were able to find dishes, glasses, bowls, a can opener, and many other things she would need when setting up her own household. Afterward they told me to have her come on Saturday at noon and that she could have anything left over from the sale.

I didn't tell her we were going to give her a bunch of stuff—I just asked if she could meet me at the church on Saturday at noon. I told her I wanted to show her something. When she arrived, I took her to the back room and showed her all of the items we had set aside for her. I thought she was going to faint. Then I shared that as soon as the sale was over, she could also have anything that was left over from the sale—free.

As the sale ended, we loaded up her little car with just about everything you can imagine. One of the men brought a trailer and delivered a computer desk and some other large items to the storage unit. Some of the men purchased a stronger lock for her.

Her little girls watched wide-eyed as their mom collected things. One of the little girls was overheard saying, "Look at all this stuff my mom is buying for us!"

As their mom continued to load up her car, one of the little girls came up to me and said, "Miss Linda, Mama is getting a lot of stuff. I don't know how she is going to pay for it. We don't have any money." I explained to the girls that their mom didn't need any money because the church was giving all of these things to them. Astonished, they said, "*What?* Everything? Why?" I said, "Because we are all family, and we love you. God loves you too, and He has led us to give you these things."

The little girls were in awe. Their mom was ecstatic and so grateful. As a matter of fact, she was afraid she was taking too much stuff until we explained that everything that was left was going to a local thrift shop.

This show of Christian love was not lost on those two little girls as they grew. It wasn't lost on the other single parents in our group. And it wasn't lost on the people in our church who contributed to help out a single-parent family in our community.

In Psalm 147:2–3 we read, "The Lord builds up Jerusalem; he gathers the exiles of Israel. He heals the brokenhearted and binds up their wounds."

If God did this for the exiles of Jerusalem, shouldn't the body of Christ today, His church, gather up

- the exiles,
- the divorced,
- the hurting,
- the widow and widower,
- the fatherless and motherless,
- the never married but raising children alone, and
- the never divorced but separated for years and raising children alone?

Allow God's example of healing broken hearts and binding up wounds to influence you. Single-parent families can belong to a complete family—a church family. It may be hard to reach out and ask for help, but hopefully thinking of the church as God's family will make it a little easier.

Lean on One Another

Single parents can find comfort in banding together. Single parents together can bear one another's burdens. As single parents, we can fulfill Galatians 6:2: "Carry each other's burdens, and in this way you will fulfill the law of Christ."

Our burdens do not automatically go away when we belong, but something amazing happens to our spirits. We find strength and support, and we realize that we are not alone; we are not the first to walk through deep waters. Through talking and sharing with others, we can find encouragement in how God has provided comfort and love for them. While in the midst of a crisis, it may be hard, if not impossible, to see life beyond the crisis or to find a solution for the dilemma. Sometimes we just need someone to "carry" our burdens for us, to walk with us through the turbulent waters.

In a church group, for example, single parents can lean on each other. Here are two testimonies:

One mom expressed that she tended to be lenient with her children when problems arose. She found it helpful to have someone to encourage her to be strong and follow through with setting boundaries for her children.

A dad said he was too strict and harsh with his child. When a problem arose, he tended to lash out and then feel sorry afterward. When this happened, he put a barrier between himself and his child. A friend helped him see that he was pushing his child away with his unyielding attitude. This friend shared how he had learned to tell his children that he would have to take time to think and pray about what had happened before he could respond to the situation.

Just through the two men sharing, talking, and eventually laughing about various situations with their children, God allowed this single dad to view his son in a different way. His parenting skills did not change overnight, but he found solace in the fact that he was not alone. There were other single dads out there, and they had developed good relationships with their children. God provided Christian brothers to help him.

"God sets the lonely in families" (Psalm 68:6).

Two Single Moms Helping Each Other

When I was single, I became friends with another single mom who had younger children. She was a counselor. We became fast friends and talked a lot, sharing our thoughts and expertise. For example, I told her when her son entered public school to be prepared for life to change. Her son would have pressure from older boys to conform to whatever the trend was. At that time—and remember this was years ago—Underoos were in style. But when boys went to first grade and used the big boys' bathroom, they were teased if they wore "preschool" underwear with a superhero or cartoon character theme. All the boys at that time were supposed to have white underwear.

One night very late she called and said, "Well, it happened tonight. After I put the boys to bed, my oldest son came out with big tears. When I asked what was wrong, he said, 'I have to have white underwear tomorrow. If I don't, the other boys will tease me and say I'm a baby because I wear baby underwear. I can't go to school tomorrow.' I was so ready for this conversation because, thanks to you, I had stocked up on white underwear and was just waiting for him to tell me he couldn't wear his cute little Underoos."

Other times I would call my friend Cindy, and she would counsel me. I was running two child care programs and needed someone to vent to who didn't work for me. She was great at listening to my rants and then calming me with her counseling abilities. It is difficult for single parents to share with other people who have no idea what it's like to operate as a single parent. Many times, we just need someone to vent to and to know we are not alone on our journey.

Church Family

As single parents, we can become part of a church family. Allow God to "set" you in a church family to fulfill some of your needs, and in turn allow yourself as a single parent to support the church family. You can bond with others by sharing your life, your laughter, your successes, and your failures also. "As with all families, commitment, struggle, laughter and shared experiences strengthen the emotional glue," writes Hoffman.[4]

When we stop focusing on our loneliness and concentrate on others the Lord puts in our path, our loneliness no longer overwhelms us. You may find moments when you are lonely, but you can come to recognize these as precious moments meant just for you. Over the years, I came to appreciate the quiet moments in my busy life. These moments were times of renewal for me. Time to rest. Time to commune intimately with my Creator. Time to laugh and connect with my precious children. Time to remember we were family.

Psalm 68:6: "God sets the lonely in families."

She wasn't . . . and then she was a part of a family.

GOING **DEEPER**

1. Take time to read the entire book of Ruth. Ask God to fill your heart with what He wants you to know about Ruth and how her and Naomi's plight can influence your life. Make notes about what you learn. Dads, this applies to you also; you can learn from Naomi's plight too.

2. Take time to study and pray about this passage:

> Praise be to the God and Father of our Lord Jesus Christ, the Father of compassion and the God of all comfort, who comforts us in all our troubles, so that we can comfort those in any trouble with the comfort we ourselves have received from God. For just as the sufferings of Christ flow over into our lives, so also through Christ our comfort overflows.
>
> 2 Corinthians 1:3–5

3. Think through this statement: "I remember a time when I didn't think I could go on for another day or minute. Then God sent _____ into my life to encourage me. They did this by _____ _____."

4. How can you use the comfort that God the Father gave you to comfort someone else? Ask God to lead you to a single parent who is struggling. Perhaps they just need a phone call. Or maybe they need comfort, food, or help solving a problem with one of their kids.

5. Can you think of someone needing encouragement or comfort right now whom you may be able to help? It helps us follow through when we put things in writing. As you pray and the Lord brings someone to mind, write about him or her below.

Name: _____

Situation: _____

How you can be of help: _____

_____

_____

6. "From him the whole body, joined and held together by every supporting ligament, grows and builds itself up in love, as each part does its work" (Ephesians 4:16).

How can you be part of the church family?
How will you allow yourself to be set in a family?
How can you reach out to others?
How can you encourage your children to reach out to others?

2

Developing a Healthy Single-Parent Family

My Home Is Not Broken

When we drove up to church one Easter Sunday morning, there was a member of the congregation outside taking pictures of all the families. As we approached the church, he motioned for us to come over and get our family picture taken. I became upset at the audacity of this man. How dare he want to take a picture of my children and me? Hadn't he heard that the children's father and I were newly divorced?

He called to us to come over and was insistent. All of a sudden, my daughter screamed, "We don't have a family!" and went running through the front door of the church. My son was quieter, but his words were just as lethal when he said, "We aren't a family anymore. Don't you know my dad left?" With his head hanging low and his shoulders slumped, he walked off in the opposite direction and through the back door of the church.

Oh my goodness, my children had just verbalized what I had been thinking, but hearing them say it hurt.

It was that Easter Sunday morning that changed the direction of our single-parent family.

All through the church service I thought about what had taken place, and after church when we got home, I sat my children down for a talk. I explained to them that we were indeed still a family. My son said, "Mom, look around. In case you haven't noticed, Dad left. We don't have a dad anymore. We're different."

I diligently explained that God still loved us and that we would need to work at being a family. I told my children that God would now be the other parent in our home. I mean, what better parent to be the father in our home than our heavenly Father?

My son, ever the practical kid, said, "Well, that's just great, but Mom, I need someone with skin on. I need somebody to talk to and someone who will answer my questions and do dad kinds of things with me." That comment threw me for a loop.

As I sat there looking at my son, thinking about what to say, the Holy Spirit filled my mind with the words to say: "Son, I hear what you are saying, but you can talk to God.

"He hears you.

"He gives you answers.

"You can hear Him in the Bible when you read it.

"You can hear Him in the sermons the preacher preaches.

"You can hear God speaking through songs and even through other people.

"You can hear Him speak to your heart and in your mind.

"And I'm sure God will provide male role models and friends who will help you become a strong Christian man."

If you are a single dad, you might have a similar conversation with your daughter. Mike Klumpp,[1] in his book *The Single Dad's Survival Guide*, tells about a time the school called him about his teen daughter. He rushed home and asked her what was wrong.

"Baby, what's wrong?"

"I started," Paige whispered. Then she began to cry.

She "started" what? Volleyball? Ahhh. *Started!* The light came on. I was totally unprepared. I had been trying to cultivate my feminine side, but this was totally outside my area of expertise. Still, as the on-duty parent, I had to do something.

Mike goes on to tell how he ran out and purchased his daughter a rose, a card, and a certificate stating she was a precious child of God. However, he never purchased the *pads* she needed. Later on, he caught his daughters giggling and asked what was going on. They proceeded to remind him of the time Paige first started her period and he only purchased a rose, a card, and a certificate. Mike took it all in his manly stride.

That Easter Sunday morning burned into my mind the importance of calling ourselves a family unit. As I began to pray, the Lord revealed to me how to create a family from the pieces that lay before me.

A Single-Parent Family or a Broken Home?

At the beginning of my single-parenting journey, my children lived in a very broken home with a very broken parent—me. I was so broken that my children didn't have a mom in their home; rather, they had a devastated and overwrought adult living with them who made mistakes and messed up many times. On that Easter Sunday morning when our friend wanted to take a family picture, the Lord took hold of me and brought me to my senses. I realized that I did have a single-parent family and it was time to act like a single parent. Thankfully, it was in time for me to step back and see what was happening.

Do your children live in a broken home or a single-parent family? There is a difference. Children from broken homes are more likely to grow up broken. Children in single-parent families have a better opportunity to grow into mature and healthy adults.

You may be questioning what the difference is between a fractured, broken home and a single-parent family.

Single-parent families are functioning units:

- There is connectedness in the relationships.
- Everyone in the family contributes to keeping the home in order. The parent assigns and the children perform chores, for example.
- There is respect and kindness between parent and child and between siblings. (Well, most of the time between the siblings. Kids are kids, and they are going to argue occasionally.)
- The parent comes across as being in charge. They provide a safe and loving home for the children.
- There is love—a love that is expressed to each other through words and actions. There is empathy. When one in the family hurts, others hurt also.

Broken homes are just that—broken:

- The people in these homes are disconnected. Everyone does their own thing. The relationships are fractured at best.
- Usually the house is in disarray because no one is in charge. The kids have few responsibilities, if any. The parent takes on all the roles of the home—cooking, cleaning, homework help, lawn maintenance, etc.
- Sometimes there is fear in these homes. Many children live in a stress-filled home. When there is a lot of stress, the child stays in the fight-or-flight part of the brain, so they are always scared. The child may never be able to tell the parent they are scared. And the parent is so stressed just trying to function that he or she is unaware the child is fearful.
- These single parents come across as malfunctioning, worn-out, combative, and beaten down. Many of them are often sighing, slumped over with an oh-poor-me look, and so exhausted.

- The parents continue to argue, and many times it is about the kids.

- Because many parents are in survival mode, they don't show love to their children through hugs, compliments, or even telling the children they love them. Also, the parent's mind is on his or her problems, and some single parents don't have empathy for the children's problems.

A family friend told me a story about a thirteen-year-old girl who took her life.[2] Her parents divorced when she was a toddler. They had a very high-conflict divorce. They fought constantly over visitation, over child support, over what could or could not happen at the other parent's home. The child was never given permission to love the other parent. When this girl turned thirteen, she had had enough. When the parents found her body, there was a suicide note that read, "You have been fighting over me my whole life. If I am no longer here, I hope you will quit fighting."

Even though the parents had been divorced for many years, each home was so broken that the child could no longer tolerate living.

Single-parent families have their ups and downs, but they stay connected. The siblings aren't always kind to each other. They have their arguments. The single parents may be grouchy or out of sorts sometimes. Overall, though, these families stay connected for the long haul.

The single parent doesn't argue with the ex-spouse. Many don't even talk to the ex-spouse.

Many times, the adults in these disconnected situations have not healed from the divorce, the death of their partner, or whatever

IF YOUR CHILDREN ARE OLD ENOUGH to make their own arrangements, allow them to connect with the other parent for pickup and drop-off times.

brought them to parenting alone. If that's the case with you, then please look into a program that will help you heal from the devastation that brought you to parenting alone. DivorceCare[3] and GriefShare[4] are two helpful programs that will assist you in your journey. I have led both programs at various churches and have seen firsthand the healing that comes from them.

What Was God's Original Design for a Family?

If we look at Genesis 2:22–24, we find His wonderful creation: "Then the Lord God made a woman from the rib he had taken out of the man, and he brought her to the man. The man said, 'This is now bone of my bones and flesh of my flesh; she shall be called "woman," for she was taken out of man.' For this reason, a man will leave his father and mother and be united to his wife, and they will become one flesh."

And Genesis 4:1–2 says, "Adam lay with his wife Eve, and she became pregnant and gave birth to Cain. She said, 'With the help of the Lord I have brought forth a man.' Later she gave birth to his brother Abel."

What a beautiful picture we see in the fourth chapter of Genesis. God designed the family to include a mother and a father. That was His original intention; however, look what happened to the first family. One brother, Cain, killed the other brother, Abel. Talk about fractured homes—that is just about as dysfunctional as it can get.

Just as the original family was broken, many families today are torn apart. You don't have to be one of those fractured or broken homes. God didn't want the first family to be fractured, and He doesn't want your family to be broken either.

I have observed many broken homes. From my observations and the study of various books, articles, and other resources, I have concluded that broken homes have certain traits.

In a spiritually and emotionally *unhealthy* broken home, the parent

- Can't cope with parenting.
- Reacts in anger toward the child(ren).
- Desires to teach the child a lesson through bribery, yelling, or trying to control the child.
- Is motivated by revenge against the other parent, God, or someone else.
- Gives little or no warning regarding punishment; the child doesn't have a chance to stop the behavior.
- Punishes the child in public or in front of friends or relatives to impress others.
- Sets the child up to fail. The parent rushes most mornings, leaves the child alone with no adult nearby, and doesn't take time to listen to the child or connect with the child.
- Offers no choices; the parent always tells the child what to do and how to do it.
- Always commands, and usually in an angry, threatening voice. "If you ever do drugs, I'll ground you for a year! Do you hear me?"
- Puts his or her own social life before the child, or the parent has no social life.
- Dotes on, hovers over, or smothers the child.
- Changes partners or lovers often.
- Is unpredictable, laughing at a behavior one day and angry over it the next.
- Allows the child to be disrespectful.
- Sets no boundaries.
- Rescues the child from consequences when the child is a toddler, preschooler, and adolescent . . . it never ends.
- Allows the child to act like an adult and take part in activities that are not age appropriate, such as dressing too maturely, smoking, drinking alcohol in the home, etc. Then this parent wonders why when these kids become adults they act like kids.

At times, parents in broken homes take on the role of victim:

- victim of divorce
- victim of death
- victim of society
- victim of their economic situation
- victim of their own children

God Can Change Victims into People Victorious in Him

Several years ago, I was conducting a weekend single-parent conference, and on Friday evening as I was leading, the Lord spoke through me. I didn't have this included in my notes and had never spoken these words before, but the following came out of my mouth: "God didn't intend for us to live in broken homes. God didn't intend for us to be victims. His plan is for us to be victorious in Him and for Him." I was thinking, *Whoa! Where did that come from?* But I went on with my talk.

After the keynote, people lined up to talk to me and ask questions. One lady, next to the last person in line, waited patiently for more than thirty people to get through visiting with me. As I approached her, she grabbed my hand and said, "I don't want to be a victim anymore. I want to be victorious in Him. How do I do that?" I said, "Let's sit down over here, and I'll tell you." I presented the plan of salvation, and she accepted Christ as her Savior.

The amazing thing about this situation was that on the way to the church, the woman who picked me up at the airport had told me about one of their single moms who was really struggling. She had a very broken home. The ministers had prayed for this mom to be at the conference that night. Before I walked out on stage, the team sponsoring the event and I prayed for this single mom to be in the audience and for the Lord to speak to her heart. And guess what? The lady who accepted Christ was the single mom we had prayed for. She became victorious through Christ.

God did indeed work in that situation and with that mom to reshape her home. He can do the same for you. He can turn your home into one that honors Him. Broken homes do not honor the Lord. To help you understand what God can do, let's go to Jeremiah 18:1–6.

What Does God's Word Say about Reshaping Our Homes?

This is the word that came to Jeremiah from the Lord: "Go down to the potter's house, and there I will give you my message." So I went down to the potter's house, and I saw him working at the wheel. But the pot he was shaping from the clay was marred in his hands; so the potter formed it into another pot, shaping it as seemed best to him.

Then the word of the Lord came to me: "O house of Israel, can I not do with you as this potter does?" declares the Lord. "Like clay in the hand of the potter, so are you in my hand."

Jeremiah 18:1–6

Notice where it says, "But the pot he was shaping from the clay was marred in his hands; so the potter formed it into another pot, shaping it as seemed best to him."

God designed the family to include a mother and a father. That was His intention, but some of our "vessels," or families, are spoiled. Allow God to be the Potter who reshapes your family into what He wants for you and your children. Put it into your mind that you are a single-parent family. Use the word *family* often when talking to and with your children.

Perhaps you have a great single-parent family already, but you need to refine it a little. Or maybe you have a broken family, and you want to turn your broken family into a healthy single-parent family. Either way, here are some things to think about and use to reshape your family.

Who Is Teaching Your Children?

Who is teaching your children values, life skills, and how to get along with other people? Most of you are going to say, "Well, I am, of course!" Let's stop and think about this for a moment. You are only one parent. If your spouse died, you might be the main influence on your child. However, if you are a single parent who is tied up in shared parenting, or your child has visitation with the other parent, or there is another parent on the scene in some way, then you are not the only one teaching your child.

Most of our children have other influences in their lives. In today's world, many of our kids are learning from social media more than we'd like to admit. Grandparents, teachers, child care workers, neighbors, friends, and our church families teach our children. Some of the learning is by observation, while some information is purposely taught. Think about who is teaching your child the following:

- A value system
- Manners
- Morals
- How to choose friends
- How to make decisions
- How to develop a good work ethic
- How to become a contributing member of society
- How to have a relationship with God
- How to be respectful of adults
- How to have integrity

I asked this same question at a retreat in Oklahoma. One single mom was downright indignant. She said, "No one teaches my child all these things but me!" I asked her,

- Does your child go to school?
- Does she ride the school bus?
- Does your little girl visit her grandparents?
- Do you take her to church—Bible study, Awana, vacation Bible school?
- Do you take her shopping with you to the grocery store, the mall, Walmart?

The mom's response was, of course, that her child did all these things, but the mom was the one teaching her values, morals, manners, etc. So, I offered the following scenario:

Let's suppose you are going someplace where you have to park in a large parking lot. You get out, lock your car, and go in the store. While you are shopping

- A man yells a cuss word close to your car.
- A woman makes a racial slur about someone.
- A couple start making out, doing some things that are inappropriate in public.
- A teen is disrespectful to her mother and screams at her.

Do any of these things affect how your car operates? Of course not, because your car is an inanimate object. It doesn't have feelings and can't be influenced. However, our children are like sponges, soaking up everything around them. If your child had been standing close by, she would have been influenced by everything that had happened. We are not the only ones teaching our children.

Take time at the end of this chapter to think about who is teaching your children all of these life skills and influencing their value system. You may have to step back and make some decisions about how you will deal with these influences.

For example, one time my son came home and said, "Mom, I don't think you would approve of some of the stuff Dad has us do." I asked, "Like what?" "Well, he put in a movie, and it had naked people in it. I knew you would not want me watching that, but I didn't know what to do because I knew Dad would get mad if I didn't watch it." I asked him what his sister did during the movie, and he said she grabbed her book and started reading.

Naturally, I wanted to storm over to his dad's and give him a piece of my mind. But I didn't, because as single parents we have no control over what goes on in the other parent's home. (Of course, if you suspect your child is being abused, neglected, molested, or hurt in any way, call the child and family services department in your state to get guidance on what to do.)

My son and I discussed the situation, and he decided he would make sure he always had a book in his backpack or a game or something to do. As single parents, we have to work extra hard at influencing our children, especially when the other parent seems to be introducing them to ideas, morals, and other things that go against our values. All you can do is pray, lead an exemplary life yourself, and depend upon the Lord to lead and guide you.

You might be asking, "How do we create emotionally and spiritually healthy single-parent homes?" The answer is we replicate Jesus. Let me repeat that: We replicate Jesus. Let's look at what we can learn from Jesus Christ our Savior when He walked on our earth.

Replicate Jesus

Everything you need to know about how to raise your kids in a single-parent home is in God's Word. Not only that, but it was modeled for us by Christ as He led His disciples and others.

Jesus taught what people should do: Love the Lord your God. He also taught that they should forgive. He always forgave. When Jesus hung on the cross after being beaten, spit upon, and tried when He had committed no crime, when He had led a sinless life, He asked the heavenly Father to forgive His accusers. "Jesus said,

IT IS ALSO IMPORTANT TO FORGIVE our former spouse. While that may seem extreme if they were the one who left and hurt you and your children, it is modeling for our children forgiveness. That doesn't mean you forget what that person did to hurt you. It does mean that you have wiped the slate clean and you move forward in your life, continuing your relationship with the heavenly Father.

'Father, forgive them, for they do not know what they are doing'" (Luke 23:34). Can we do anything less for our own children?

He also had empathy for people in various situations—something many single parents struggle with, especially when it comes to ex-spouses or extended families.

Jesus was gentle but firm at the same time. He taught that there are consequences for actions. He also taught that there are consequences for failing to take action.

He was tender and caring for the weak and for the hurting. He cared deeply.

Jesus pulled the children onto His lap. In other words, He gave physical attention to them. It is something many children want and need. When did you last hug your kid? He also honored children by allowing them to contribute—think of the boy with the loaves and fishes. Imagine the honor that boy felt when he contributed to the entire community.

Jesus came down to our level. He spoke to us so we could understand. He ate with His disciples. They spent mealtimes together. Single-parent families desperately need to find time to have at least one meal together each day and not be rushing, watching TV, or using social media.

He walked and talked. You might say He made the most of each moment, even when traveling. Know when many kids talk

FOR ME, many times that time away was in the bathroom. Even then my son would lie down on the floor and speak through the crack under the door. My kids were talkers!

freely? In the car—but not with movies on or handheld devices or iPhones engaged.

Jesus was not afraid to discipline. He publicly rebuked Peter when he was out of line. He also brought up secret, uncomfortable subjects. He asked, "What were you arguing about?" when His disciples discussed who was to be first (Mark 9:33).

Again, He showed physical attention. Not only did children sit in His lap, but the disciples leaned against Him at the Last Supper as they reclined to eat. He was also not afraid to show emotion in front of them. He expressed joy and sadness; He cried, showed anger, frustration, etc. We should not shield our children from our emotions. We should, however, display them appropriately.

Jesus taught His disciples and gave them small assignments to test their abilities, then corrected their errors. He not only said, "Do what I say" but also "Do what I do." He led by example when He washed the feet of those around Him.

He directed them to people they could trust when He was gone: "'Dear woman, here is your son,' and to the disciple, 'Here is your mother'" (John 19:26–27).

He showed them that even a leader needs time alone as He would slip away and pray. Yes, even single parents need time away to pray, contemplate, and read God's Word.

Traits of a Successful Single-Parent Family

Replicate Jesus, and it won't be long before you'll begin to see a single-parent family emerging. Here are just a few traits of an emotionally and spiritually healthy single-parent family:

1. The parent sets up schedules that are consistent but flexible. As kids age, schedules need to change.

   I love how Robert Beeson explains his daily schedule in the book *Going Solo*.

   > Before I knew it, the alarm blast would summon me to get out of bed, brush my teeth, and brace myself for the morning circus that daily paraded its three-ring fun into the kitchen. All three girls were in school, so the first hour awake required a lot of prep in a short window of time. Each day by 6:15-ish, I was acting as . . .
   >
   > - Hair stylist (No, Daddy! That's not how the braid is supposed to look!)
   > - Caterer (Honey, be patient, I'm cooking breakfast *while* I'm making your lunch.)
   > - Fashion consultant (No, I mean it, babe. That dress *still* looks beautiful on you.)
   > - Drama coach (I'm sure your friend wasn't trying to be mean to you and, by the way, we don't use that word.)
   > - Paramedic (No, Daddy, *I* have the hangnail. *Zoe* needs the Band-Aid for her knee.)
   > - Priest (Yes, before you all leave for school, we will pray for the hamster.)[5]

2. Each member of the family unit is recognized as valuable.
3. Each person contributes by shouldering responsibilities that promote the well-being of the family.
4. Family members communicate with each other; everyone has a chance to contribute to the conversation, and consideration is given to what the parent has to say as well.
5. Family members support one another by attending kids' school events when possible. Children also attend events with the parent.

   I had my son and his friend attend summer concerts in the park with me. Did they like it? Not really, but they

IF FAMILIES ARE RUSHED with teens and parents going in different directions, set up a communication journal.

Every evening when the kids go to bed they can write in their own journal and leave it in a designated place for the next morning.

Mom or Dad reads the journal during the day, answers any questions or makes comments, and returns it in the evenings.

I encourage the paper journal rather than an electronic device because I believe all electronic devices should be turned in to the parent at some point in the evening. Also, no child should have access to any social media in their bedroom alone at night. I've known of a single parent who took all electronics and locked them in the trunk of her car—this after she caught her young son looking at porn. Do what you have to do so kids can get a good night's sleep and not be on any games or social media.

went because I was the mom and insisted that my son accompany me.

We all went to programs at church or to the movies as a family. We went to the school band concerts and to parades the kids marched in with their band.

It is important that all are trustworthy; if you say you are going to do something with your children, then do it. Don't disappoint your children by not showing up or by cancelling because of something more important. To a child there is nothing more important than the trust between you and them.

6. The parent is reliable and consistent. You, as the parent, must model being consistently reliable in your daily life. Be and do what you say you are going to do. In other words, if you say Saturday morning you are making pancakes, you need to make sure you make pancakes. We all

have interruptions, and when that happens, an explanation needs to be given every time.

7. All are respectful. All family members, including the parent, respect each other. In some situations, the parent is going to have to model respect.

One time I heard my daughter utter a swear word. I was upstairs, and she was at the bottom of the stairs. I guess she thought I couldn't hear. I came to the upstairs landing and said, "Julie, there is no swearing in this house."

My son said, "Mom, everybody cusses. You can't be with us all the time, so how do you know we are cussing or not?"

I replied, "What you say is true. I can't be with you 24/7, nor do I want to. However, you need to know that there are three places I expect you two to be respectful enough not to swear. And those places are 1) in my home; 2) in front of your grandmother; and 3) at church.

"Anywhere else I hope you have the good sense to consider your surroundings and the consequences of what might happen to you if you swear. I'm thinking of the school bus and class."

8. The adult shows appropriate emotions for various situations. My kids saw me cry more than once. And they saw me get angry and frustrated.

9. All family members contribute to society.

- For younger children, their society is the home. Even young children need to be encouraged to take part in chores and housekeeping.

- Blogger and author Tim Elmore, in his blog post "The Research on What Creates Satisfied and Successful Kids,"[6] says that according to a Harvard study[7] there is a close tie between successful grown-ups and childhood chores. So put those kids to work in your home. Children take ownership when they contribute.

10. The family reads God's Word and prays together.

> You shall therefore lay up these words of mine in your
> heart and in your soul; and you shall bind them as a sign
> upon your hand, and they shall be as frontlets between
> your eyes. And you shall teach them to your children, talk-
> ing of them when you are sitting in your house, and when
> you are walking by the way, and when you lie down, and
> when you rise. And you shall write them upon the door-
> posts of your house and upon your gates, that your days
> and the days of your children may be multiplied in the
> land which the Lord swore to your fathers to give them, as
> long as the heavens are above the earth.
>
> Deuteronomy 11:18–21 (RSV)

11. The family sets up new rituals and continues some rituals and traditions from the past.
12. The family solves problems together.
13. Family members share leisure time; they play, laugh, and share humor together.

    In our home, we laughed a lot. We did silly and fun things. We jumped on the beds and over the couches and ran down the stairs, and I'm sure if our neighbors had looked in the windows, they would have thought I had finally lost it.

    One time my daughter had a friend over to spend the night. They decided to have a *Planet of the Apes* marathon. We sat up way into the night watching every *Planet of the Apes* movie ever made. At one point my son climbed up on the couch and went to sleep. I don't know what time I fell asleep, but I woke up the next morning on the floor with sunlight streaming in on my face. The TV was blaring away, and my daughter and her friend were asleep on the floor. Popcorn bowls, sodas, and other snack foods were strewn across the floor. I sat up smiling and praising God we had spent the night laughing and having a good time. All because of the *Planet of the Apes* movie marathon.

How are you doing? Are you leaning more into the lifestyle of a single-parent family?

What Does God's Word Say?

To help you change from a broken home to a single-parent family, read Colossians 3. Verses 5–11 tell you what to do to change your parenting.

Put to death, therefore, whatever belongs to your earthly nature: sexual immorality, impurity, lust, evil desires and greed, which is idolatry. Because of these, the wrath of God is coming. You used to walk in these ways, in the life you once lived. But now you must rid yourselves of all such things as these: anger, rage, malice, slander, and filthy language from your lips. Do not lie to each other, since you have taken off your old self with its practices and have put on the new self, which is being renewed in knowledge in the image of its Creator. Here there is no Greek or Jew, circumcised or uncircumcised, barbarian, Scythian, slave or free, but Christ is all, and is in all.

Colossians 3:12–14 describes a parent who is creating a home where children will grow up in a healthy environment.

Therefore, as God's chosen people, holy and dearly loved, clothe yourselves with

- compassion,
- kindness,
- humility,
- gentleness and
- patience.

Bear with each other and forgive whatever grievances you may
have against one another.
Forgive as the Lord forgave you.
And over all these virtues put on love, which binds them all
together in perfect unity.

(Bullets and paragraph breaks added for emphasis)

Your children do not have to come from an unhealthy broken
home. They can be raised in a single-parent family. Be the parent
God intended you to be. Ideally, each of us should have the relationship with our child that God wants to have with us.

Remember that Satan is a liar. He will try to destroy our single-
parent, Christian homes. If you remember, Genesis 3:1 states that
the serpent, Satan, was crafty. Adam and Eve had the perfect family. Satan told Eve to eat of the forbidden tree and said that she
would surely not die. Eve did eat from the forbidden tree, and later
on she died. Don't let Satan destroy your family.

Stay close to God and to the Lord's family—the church. Don't
listen to the evil one when he wants you to feel defeated because
you feel you are the only parent in your situation. Whether you are
a single mom or a single dad, you are not the only parent—you are
the other parent alongside God, our heavenly Parent.

A Lasting Impact

Remember the story we started with? The one where I had the
discussion with my son about God being the father in our home?
Brian was in the second grade when that happened. When he was
going into his senior year of high school I decided I needed to have
a sit-down talk with him. Little did I know how much what was
said back then had impacted him.

Me: "Brian, I'm a little worried about you hanging around with
Chris. He seems to be getting into a lot of trouble lately."

Brian: "Mom, Chris is my friend. Remember when I was in
second grade and we had that talk about God being the father in

our home? You told me to talk to God and He would listen. Well, that night I went to bed, and I told God I was really lonely and I needed a friend. The next day Chris showed up in our class. We have been friends for ten years. I know God brought him into my life. I know he is having problems and getting into trouble, but we have been best friends for ten years and I won't desert him now."

Me: "Wow! I had no idea. I trust your judgment, son. Just be careful, and don't let him get you into trouble."

To be honest with you, I was so proud of that kid. He had taken to heart what I had said. He had studied God's Word. And he had matured enough to make the complicated decision to stick by his best friend.

Who knew that a conversation with a seven-year-old would impact him for years to come? God knew. I have no doubt that God knew. As a follow-up, both boys graduated from high school. Both boys have gone on to lead exemplary adult lives. My son is a doctor in Texas. Chris has had a very successful career also.

GOING DEEPER

1. Stop and think for a minute about what you see in your mind when you hear the term *broken home*. Write down those words and then cross out the ones that don't describe your home.

   Read Jeremiah 18:1–6 and consider the following:

   • How can God, the Potter, change your home?
   • What are some things you need to do to create an emotionally and spiritually healthy home?
   • How are you going to enjoy your home?

2. Kids need a place to call their home. A place where they belong. Where they can lay down their worries and

burdens and just be enclosed in their space. Children's personal space is important to their well-being. How will you allow each of your children to develop or design their personal space? (For example, in our home we went to the

HERE ARE TEN TIPS TO HELP a noncustodial parent set up their home for visitation every other weekend.[8]

1. Be ready for your children. In other words, have their favorite foods on hand or some of their favorite games, books, a bed, and a place for their things.
2. Develop a ritual for when they arrive or when you pick them up. Maybe a high five, head rub, or fist bump—something they can come to depend upon. Any interaction between you and the child is good. If there is more than one child, then develop a hello ritual for each one.
3. Develop a good-bye ritual also. Kids need to understand and know you are saying good-bye, and you are connecting with them. This way, they will come to know you are always there even when you have to say good-bye at the end of the visit.
4. Have some sort of schedule. In other words, get up at the same time each time they visit; go to bed at approximately the same time. A schedule allows the child to know what's coming next. It doesn't have to be strict.
5. Before they leave, talk about what they'd like to do next time they visit (e.g., rent a movie, go see a movie, wash the car, or go swimming). This will give them something to look forward to at your home.
6. Set up your place like a home—a second home for them. Have a place to put their clothes, toothbrush, etc. Keep a toothbrush, soap, deodorant, pj's, and extra clothes and underwear at your home. Even if you have to go purchase

paint store, and each kid got to pick a paint color for their room. I helped each child paint their room.)

3. If your children live in two homes, encourage them to talk with the other parent about what they need in the other

these items, kids need to know that you care enough to prepare for them, and that you want them with you.

7. Develop a bedtime ritual, even if your kids are older—and even if it's just eating a bowl of cereal together. For a deeper bedtime ritual, after the cereal, read Scripture each night they are with you. Read something that is uplifting and lets them know that God loves them very much.

8. Ask about the children's schoolwork when they are in school. If they have a test coming up, have them bring their spelling words or books to read to your home, and help them study. It might only be half an hour, but this says you care about their life and want to be involved in it.

9. Have chores to do at your home. Even if it's nothing more than making the bed and emptying the trash, kids feel like they belong when they contribute to the home. Though they are only there a couple of days, they still need to contribute. It might be loading the dishwasher, being responsible for helping cook the meals, or vacuuming the place where they sleep. You can do chores together to bring harmony and connectedness to your kids. Think about washing the car or some other chore that can be turned into a fun event.

10. Enjoy yourself, and have fun, but be a parent. Don't be the fun, weekend parent—just be the parent God intends you to be. Love your children, laugh with them, cry with them, cheer them up, and keep up a good attitude toward the other parent.

home. While you have no control over what happens in the other home, it's important that your child be able to communicate with the other parent. If you have a good relationship with your ex-spouse, then talk about how each parent can help your children feel safe and comfortable in their living spaces.

3

Behavior and Discipline Issues

The Lord Is My Shepherd . . . but Who Is Going to Help Me Raise These Kids?

I came home from work one day when my son was thirteen years old to find him in the den lifting weights. Ever since his dad had moved out five years before, he had been on a quest to build strong, manly muscles. Of course, that's pretty hard to do when you are only eight years old and the testosterone had not kicked in yet. Even the pediatrician had explained to him why his muscles wouldn't bulk up when he was eight. But now he was thirteen. With his muscles starting to bulge, he said, "Mom, look! I'm getting pretty strong."

As I took off my jacket and put my purse down, I said, "Yes, you are, son."

He then said, "Actually, I'm taller than you now. I'm stronger than you now." And with a slight little grin he said, "And really, now that I'm stronger than you, there is nothing you can make me do."

With a big grin on my face, I said, "Son, son. There is an old proverb in our family that I guess you have never heard. The saying is 'He who rules the money rules the world.' And I happen to rule the money in your world. Therefore, I rule you." My smile widened.

He replied, "Well, when I'm sixteen I'll get a job, and I'll rule my own world."

To which I responded, "And I'll charge you rent, and I'll still rule your world." We both had a good chuckle as I hugged him.

Now why would I start off a chapter about behavior and discipline issues with a story like this one?

Because I want you to see and understand that the key to behavior and discipline issues is relationship. You can't discipline a child you don't have a relationship with, and relationship means more than giving commands, yelling, and screaming. Relationship means that you bond with your child. You have empathy, understanding, and even tenderness in some situations.

Don't get me wrong—I don't mean you need to be a wimp and let the kids run all over you.

My son and I had a good relationship. He was testing the waters a bit about his strength to see how I would handle him being physically stronger and bigger than I am. I opted to use humor to get my point across that I was still the adult and the parent in the home. I could have threatened him with "Oh yeah? That's what you think, young man! I'm still the parent in this house, and you'll do what I say. I don't care how big you are." Or I could have made fun of him: "Oh sure, with those little bumps on those scrawny arms. Ha! I doubt it." Instead, I handled it with grace and humor that brought us a little closer together.

He was still a kid, and every so often a kid has to test the waters to see if you are still in charge.

Disclaimer

If you are looking for rules and specific ways to discipline in a situation, you will not find that in this book. That type of household is a cold, rule-based atmosphere and not a loving home. Every situation with your children is different and will need to be addressed differently. For example, let's say your kid slams the door when he comes in from outside. If you have a rule-based home that says, "Every time you slam the door, you will go to your room and stay until I call you," you have no choice but to send him to his room. But what if the wind caught the door and he wasn't strong enough to keep it from slamming? What if he has grown a lot lately, and he comes running in to tell you something exciting? Or the smart-alecky kid down the street said something ugly about his sister, and he is beside himself about what to say to this kid and is so upset he didn't realize he slammed the door?

You need to find out why the door slammed and deal with it from that point. When my son was a certain age, it seemed like every door he opened he slammed shut or it slammed into the wall. We sat down and talked about it. I told him that he needed to be aware of the wind outside, and if it was windy he'd need to know that the wind could catch the door and slam it into the wall. If that happened and the doorknob knocked a hole in the wall, he would have to patch the wall.

Sure enough, it was only a couple of weeks and there was a hole in the wall. "Mom, I'm sorry. It was really windy, and the wind caught the door." I was sorry that happened too, but I had warned him and now he'd have to repair the hole. He explained he didn't know how to do that. My reply: "Bummer. Better figure it out. Let me know what you'll need to fix that hole and I'll get it for you."

Parenting Alone Is Not Impossible

Parenting alone is a difficult task but not an impossible task. I want to encourage you to go to the Scriptures and find divine guidance for parenting in particular situations. More than once I have pored over the Scriptures looking for guidance for a particular incident.

We can learn from the Twenty-third Psalm general parenting guidelines. In this psalm we learn we all have a Shepherd to guide us along this single-parent journey. We have a Shepherd who protects us and who soothes our hurts. We can learn from the Shepherd and from God's Word about raising our children alone.

> The Lord is my shepherd, I shall not be in want.
> He makes me lie down in green pastures,
> he leads me beside quiet waters, he restores my soul.
> He guides me in paths of righteousness for his name's sake.
> Even though I walk through the valley of the shadow of death,
> I will fear no evil, for you are with me;
> your rod and your staff, they comfort me.
> You prepare a table before me in the presence of my enemies.
> You anoint my head with oil; my cup overflows.
> Surely goodness and love will follow me all the days of my life,
> and I will dwell in the house of the Lord forever.
>
> Psalm 23

I think we can all agree that parenting alone can wear us down. It is exhausting mentally, emotionally, and even spiritually. Go back over this passage while lying in a quiet spot outside or sitting in a quiet place. Imagine, if you will, lying down in green pastures. Take a moment to exhale as you think about the Lord guiding you every step of the way. Feel the cool, green grass under you. Imagine the cool, quiet waters restoring your soul and refreshing your spirit. Trust the Shepherd as He walks along the paths of righteousness.

Fear nothing as you face your enemies because Satan, your biggest enemy, wants you to fail. He wants your kids to get into drugs, alcohol, and early sexual activity. He wants your kids to be disrespectful, arrogant, lazy, and, in general, little brats.

Let's take a look at the rod and staff mentioned in verse four: "Even though I walk through the valley of the shadow of death, I will fear no evil, for you are with me; your rod and your staff, they comfort me." Shepherds used the rod to fight off wild beasts of the field. It was also used to tap the side of the ground next to the sheep so the sheep would stay on the pathway. This was particularly useful when sheep were traveling on narrow pathways on high mountains. Tap, tap, tap. The shepherd tapped back and forth between the sides of the cliff.

On the end of the staff was a crook that was used to pull a sheep back to safety if one fell or slipped over the side. The rod and staff comforted the sheep because they meant the shepherd was there and they were protected and guided.[1]

If we apply this line of thinking to our situation as parents, and if we think of ourselves as the shepherd and our discipline and guidance as the rod and staff, then we can realize that our children are comforted and feel secure with us as parents.

There will be times you will need to warn your children about upcoming dangers or about staying on the right pathway. Tap, tap, tap from different sides as you gently guide them along.

One of the rules in my home was if you wanted to spend the night someplace or have a friend come spend the night in our home, then I had to meet the child's parents. This was one of those tap, tap, taps.

I wanted to protect my children even—and especially—when they were teens. I had to know if the home where one of them would spend the night was a safe place. I had to know that the parents were going to be home. I realize you can't always be sure after a few visits and a couple of phone calls, but at least it gave me an opportunity to have a little understanding about the situation. Mostly, my kids spent the night with church families or families in our community, and I either knew the other family or I knew someone who knew them.

There will be other times you may have to reach out, pull them back up, and rescue them from a potential danger, such as drugs, sexting, lying, cheating at school, etc. There are tough calls, and you'll have to stay calm, pray before you address the situation, and possibly even get some advice from a counselor or someone you trust. Luckily for me, I had a friend who was a youth counselor, and more than once I talked a situation over with him, especially when I had custody of my teenage great-nephew.

One thing I don't advocate for single parents, and that is spanking your child. The reason? You are alone, and there is no one to calm you down or keep you from losing your temper. Let's face it—there are times when you might get angry or upset. I fear if you opt to use spanking as a punishment, you may get out of control and hurt your child.

Have you ever wondered if

- You are too lenient?
- You are too strict?
- You are too inconsistent?

Let's discuss what discipline actually means. It will help you learn more about your parenting.

What Is Discipline?

The word *discipline* comes from the same word as *disciple*. When you look in *Merriam-Webster Unabridged* under the word *discipline* it refers you to the word *disciple*.[2] What did the disciples do in the Bible? They taught, helped people, healed people, spread the word about Christ's miracles, and listened to and learned from Jesus. They had empathy for people in a sinful world. They tried to understand various situations. They loved people.

Discipline involves the following:

- **Helping** children learn how to get along with family, friends, and society. A family is the child's first society. It's where he learns how to act and behave out in the world.

56

- **Teaching** children to behave in an agreeable way and in accordance with the laws of the land. The first law of the land is in your home, the second is in the school and community, and the third, which they learn as young adults, is in the country in which we live.
- **Encouraging** children to learn self-control so that the child wants to do what is right because of how she feels under her skin and inside her body, not just to avoid getting caught.
- **Empathizing** with your child.
- **Loving** your child unconditionally.

Instead of asking if you are too lenient, too strict, or too inconsistent, ask yourself these questions:

- Am I helping my child learn to get along?
- Am I teaching my child what I expect and how to behave in different situations?
- Am I encouraging my child to be all he can be, to use the talents and skills God has given him?
- Do I have empathy for my child in all situations? Do I try to understand where my child is coming from and what happened to cause her to act like this?
- Do I love my child unconditionally as the Savior loves me?
- Am I fair to my child?

When my fifteen-year-old great-nephew came to live with me, my daughter had already joined the military. She sent him a note that said, "My mom is tough but she is fair. She only wants what's best for you." Kids know if you are fair to them. Being fair doesn't mean you treat each child the same way. Each child needs to be dealt with individually. Being fair means you take into consideration all of the issues surrounding a particular incident.

Do You Know Your Child as God Knows You?

Let's go to Psalm 139 and learn how well God knows you. "O Lord, you have searched me and you know me. You know when I sit and when I rise; you perceive my thoughts from afar. You discern my going out and my lying down; you are familiar with all my ways. Before a word is on my tongue you know it completely, O Lord. . . . For you created my inmost being; you knit me together in my mother's womb" (Psalm 139:1–4, 13).

Isn't it amazing that God knows us so well? He knows what annoys you. He knows what bores you and what energizes you. He knows what kinds of stories and movies make you cry and the types of jokes that make you laugh uproariously. He knows what affects you and stresses you. He knows every single thing about you before you even know it yourself.

Ponder your answers to the following questions.

Do you know your child as well as God knows you?

Do you know when your child rises and sleeps, or who their friends are?

Do you know how they are feeling about different things, including politics, rules at school, God?

Do you know your child's learning style? There are several learning styles, but for our purposes, let's just look at the three major ones.

1. Auditory—an auditory learner uses spoken words.
2. Visual—a visual learner prefers written words, pictures, images.
3. Kinesthetic—this type of learner prefers using their hands, body, and sense of touch.

Why would it be important for you to know your child's learning style? For me it made communicating much easier. For instance,

ONE MORNING WHEN MY KIDS WERE TEENS, they were both in my bathroom getting ready for school. Don't ask me why because they had a bathroom they shared. I watched as my son picked up a bottle of water, looked at his sister, and then sprayed his hair. She yelled, "Hey, why didn't you tell me you were going to spray water?" He said, "I looked at you!" This is a perfect example of two very different learners.

my daughter is an auditory learner. Just tell her something once, and she is good to go. My son, on the other hand, is a visual learner and had to have lists made out for his chores.

It is important for you to know your child like God knows you. In order for this to happen, you must connect with your child on a regular basis. Being on your iPhone or iPad is not connecting with your child. Listen to yourself one evening. If you hear yourself saying, "Uh-huh. Just a minute until I get this message read." *Type, type, type.* "Now what were you saying?" *Twiddle, twiddle.* "Wait. I have to answer Grandma." *Type, type, type.* This is not connecting with your child.

Experts strongly suggest we bring back the family meal. I think this is an important concept in single-parent families. This is a time that is relaxed and when you can get to know what your kids have been up to or what they are doing. It's also a time when you can share with your kids about your day.

When you are at the table eating, all electronics need to be turned off or put away. This is your time to connect. I know one single mom who had a rule for dinner. Each night everyone, including her, had to tell one good thing that happened during that day. She knew her kids' friends well enough to ask questions about them. Employing this tactic, I might ask, "So, Brian, how was Chris today? What did his mom say about him flunking that spelling test?"

There were many times I used other children's situations to teach my kids. "Chris flunked his spelling test? Do you know what will happen to you if you should flunk your spelling test because you didn't study?" I learned a lot about my kids' friends. I knew who didn't have to do housework, who lied to their parents, who said what in band or on the playground. You'll be amazed at what you learn.

This is one time that the single parent has an advantage over a married couple. When I was a single parent, all of my attention at dinner went to the kids. When I was married, there was another adult in the home who wanted my attention. So take advantage of this time to learn more about your children.

Good discipline for your kids depends on having a relationship with them and knowing them well, as God knows you. When you know your kids as well as God knows you, you naturally develop an instinct and understanding about them. This is also known as intuition.

Activate Your Intuition

When you know your child well, you develop intuition about your kid and what she or he is up to. For example, one New Year's Eve my daughter went to spend the night with her best friend. She had left early in the afternoon. At about five o'clock, something didn't feel right about it, so I called this best friend's mom. I asked how she was, and what the girls were doing. She proceeded to tell me that the girls had just left a few minutes ago with their dates to go to the movies. Dates? *Dates???* My daughter was only fifteen. We had an agreement that she wouldn't date in a car until she was fifteen and a half, which was not until February.

After calming down, I called back and asked to which movie theater they had gone. I had a date that night to go to the Methodist church's New Year's Eve dance. I called my date and told him we'd have to make a detour. I called my ex-mother-in-law and asked if my daughter could spend the night at her house. Then I went to the theater to find my daughter. I tapped her on the shoulder and crooked my finger for her to follow me.

After allowing her to go back and tell her friends good-bye, I took her to her grandmother's house. Once in the car, she tried to explain, to which I responded, "Right now might not be a good time to talk about this. We'll talk later." The next morning my son and I lay around the house watching movies. Finally, at around one in the afternoon he said, "Mom, where's Julie?" I just said she was at Grandma's house and we'd go get her later. I didn't tell him she was in trouble. It wasn't any of his business.

At around four in the afternoon we picked up my daughter. I said nothing about what had happened. Life went on as usual. I wasn't mad or upset. See, I knew the worst punishment for a teenage girl was having to spend the night at her grandmother's on a holiday with no makeup, no hairbrush, no toothbrush, no deodorant, no change of clothes, and no access to a phone.

After three days she came to me and said, "Mom, when are we going to talk? This is killing me. What's my punishment for disobeying you?" I told her that she had punished herself, because she had chosen to lie to me, and when she lied she had chosen to have a break in our relationship. It was a hard lesson for her. For me? Not so much, because my life had gone on as usual and wasn't disrupted.

A COUPLE OF YEARS LATER my son came home from middle school talking about how physically affectionate the kids were in his school. I said, "I better not ever hear about you kissing a girl in the hall at school." To which his sister added, "Yeah, because Mom will march up to that school and embarrass you in front of all your friends when she pulls you out of class." Ha, ha! I used one kid to teach the other kid!

How Do I Do This Parenting Thing Alone?

"Give me now wisdom and knowledge to go out and come in before this people, for who can rule this thy people, that is so great?" (2 Chronicles 1:10 RSV). Your people as a single parent are your children. God can and will give you wisdom and knowledge when you ask Him.

Let's talk about some methods you can use to do this parenting thing alone.

Try the step-back parenting method

When something happens—*stop*, *think*, and *step back*. Literally make yourself take a step back. It is a physical movement that can give you time to think. Instead of reacting as many of us do, you need to take time to think through a situation. Tell your child you'll get back to him when you've had time to think about things. I usually took an entire day to think things through. If it was a big decision, then I took longer. This helped me to be fair to my kids.

One time I was conducting a single-parent workshop and telling about the step-back parenting method, and one dad said, "Oh man, if I had used this last Friday night, I would have had to walk backward a block!" After we all laughed, he went on to share how his daughter had gotten arrested for being drunk and disorderly. He had reacted by cursing at her and mumbling the entire drive to get his kid out of jail. After thinking about it for a minute, he said, "Yeah, I get how if I had stopped in the moment, stepped back, and collected myself, I wouldn't have reacted the way I did. The only thing I taught her that night was how to lose her temper and yell."

In my home one of the rules was if you wanted to go spend the night with a friend, you had to ask at least twenty-four hours in advance. If you didn't ask in advance, then the answer was an automatic "No!" The reason I needed twenty-four hours' notice was because I wanted to check out the situation. I wanted to make sure things were safe and as they were supposed to be. I wanted to know who was in charge and what was going to be taking place. I didn't have to worry about stepping back often or even regretting situations because I had set the rules early on.

Use positive motivation

Positive motivation is when you work in an upbeat and positive way to influence your kids. Some tips for positive motivation:

- Inspire your child at every age toward their best effort.
- Spend time together—build relationships and have fun.
- Praise good behavior by being descriptive. "You put the dishes in the dishwasher without being asked. That was helpful." Do not use the words "good job" or "good boy," as they are not descriptive, don't teach, and generally are used so often they don't really mean much.
- Use the phrase "You are doing it." Or "You are doing it; you are putting your sock on." Being positive with the child and saying "You're doing it" gives them a shot of serotonin in the brain. Serotonin is the feel-good chemical that is released when one is affirmed.
- Give choices; choices empower children.

  o Preschool kids: "Do you want to wear the red shirt or the blue shirt tomorrow?"
  o Elementary kids: "Do you want to take your lunch or buy your lunch at school on Monday?"
  o Teens: "Are you driving to school or riding the bus?" (Okay, that might not be much of a choice because we know most teens will want to drive.) "Are you going to play a sport this year or play in the band?"

- Use incentives—"When we get our work done we can watch a movie together."

I'D ENCOURAGE YOU NOT TO USE REWARD SYSTEMS such as stickers for younger children. Reward systems teach "other" control. In other words, a child does something to please the adult so they can get a reward. These are the kids who go into the teen years trying to please everyone. Do you really want that fifteen-year-old daughter in the back of a car only wanting to please her boyfriend by engaging in sex? Do you really want that fourteen-year-old son trying to please the kids offering him the drug of their choice?

- Celebrate the big events such as graduating from high school, making the soccer team, etc. Do not celebrate every little accomplishment, but save celebrations for life-changing events.

Parenting becomes very simplified if we take time to realize that we can pattern our parenting skills after the best parent of all—our heavenly Father. Think about how God parents us. He sets boundaries, guidelines, and laws with consequences. And yet He doesn't force us to believe in Him. He doesn't even force us to obey His laws. The consequences are pretty severe for many of the laws we break, but He still allows us to make our own choices.

Set up boundaries and guidelines

Boundaries and guidelines give children direction. They lay out what is expected and what is accepted.

To help you understand the why of boundaries, let's take a little trip. Let's say that we have to go to an appointment. We leave the house in plenty of time. There are two different routes we can take. Each is a dark stretch of a country road. It is night, and we are alone. Just as we leave the house it begins to rain.

The first road has clearly defined lanes marked with bright stripes. When the road becomes narrow with deep culverts and ditches on the side, there are guardrails and wide shoulders. There are signs indicating sharp curves and clearly marked no-passing zones where needed. As you travel along, you notice speed-limit signs giving you an idea of how fast you can safely travel. You notice a sign ahead indicating there is an intersection coming up with a traffic light and you may have to stop. Then you notice street signs telling you where you are.

The second road is quite different. This road has a faded center line, and you are not exactly sure where your side of the road begins and ends. As your car climbs the hill, you suspect that there are deep ditches along the side of the road, but you don't see any guardrails. There are no shoulders along the side of the road, just steep cliffs. As the road narrows and curves, you look for traffic signs indicating when the next curve will appear, but you only see faded, unrecognizable signs. There's no warning of an upcoming intersection, and there are no posted speed limits.

Most of us will choose to travel the road that has clearly marked boundaries. When we choose to travel the road with boundaries we feel safe; we have clear expectations of what's to come and where we are going.

- The brightly marked lanes are boundaries.
- The guardrails are boundaries that keep us from going over the edge into a steep cliff.
- Speed limits give us boundaries as to what speed we can travel.
- No-passing zones give us clear boundaries to keep us and the other cars safe.

The same holds true for children. They need boundaries to

- feel safe,
- have clear expectations of what's to come,

- understand what's expected of them, and
- know where they are going.

Children from single-parent families in particular need their parents to set clear boundaries. Many times, our children have to follow different sets of rules—our rules and the rules at the other parent's home. We cannot control what takes place at the other home, but we can take control over what occurs at our own home. As part of our boundaries discussion, let me ask you a question. What do you want for your child or children when they become adults? (Write your answers in the "Going Deeper" section.) What are your dreams for your child? What are your plans?

For a long time, I literally couldn't think that far ahead. I was busy just trying to survive. My first prayer when I became single was, *God, don't let Julie get pregnant, and don't let Brian get into drugs.* Julie was eleven years old, and Brian was seven. I bought into all the hype about children from broken homes. As long as I embraced that line of thinking, my children were doomed. I found myself thinking, *Why try? They're from a broken home. They don't have a chance.*

Then I realized that I, their mother, was training them just as you are training your child right now. There is no one else in your home. You are the parent.

Jane Nelsen, in her book *Positive Discipline for Single Parents*, writes:

> It's a myth that children living with single parents are automatically more deprived than children living with two parents. . . . Many happy, successful people have been raised by divorced parents, widows, or widowers—or even in orphanages. It is not the circumstances of life, but the way we perceive those circumstances that has the greatest impact. Each person decides whether challenges will be stumbling blocks or stepping stones to joy and success.[3]

The Bible says in Proverbs 22:6, "Train a child in the way he should go, and when he is old he will not turn from it."

In order to train a child, we need to look ahead. Ask yourself these questions:

- What road signs or boundaries am I putting up for my children?
- What is the direction I want them to go?
- What am I doing to point them in that direction?
- How am I preparing them for the bumps and detours that are waiting for them?

In the book *Boundaries with Kids*, Dr. Henry Cloud and Dr. John Townsend observed, "In 1992 we wrote *Boundaries*, a book about taking control of one's life," and as they worked with adults, they realized that boundary problems had not developed in their adult years.

They had learned patterns early in life and then continued with out-of-control patterns in their adult lives, where the stakes were higher. They had learned the following boundary problems as youngsters:

- Inability to say no to hurtful people or set limits on hurtful behavior from others
- Inability to say no to their own destructive impulses
- Inability to hear no from others and respect their limits
- Inability to delay gratification and accomplish goals and tasks
- Tendency to be attracted to irresponsible or hurtful people and then try to "fix" them
- Taking responsibility for other people's lives
- Ability to be easily manipulated or controlled
- Struggles with intimacy and maintaining closeness with others
- Inability to be honest with those they are close to
- Inability to confront others and resolve conflicts productively

67

- Experiencing life as a victim instead of living it purposefully with a feeling of self-control
- Addictions and compulsions
- Disorganization and lack of follow-through[4]

Teach responsibility

Let's go back to the question we asked a few minutes ago and rephrase it a little. What is it that you really want for your children? Do you want them to grow up to be healthy, happy adults, contributing to society?

Remember my first prayer as a single parent? *Oh God, don't let Julie get pregnant and Brian get into drugs.* As I healed from my divorce, studied God's Word, and researched information on parenting alone, I began to take control of my life. I began to think about what I really wanted for my children and what I didn't want for them. Each of us will have different ideas about what we want for our children.

One of the character traits I wanted my children to possess was responsibility. I didn't want them to be dependent on me for the rest of their lives. I went from that pitiful prayer about pregnancy and drugs to making the decision that when my children turned eighteen they would be responsible enough that they would no longer have a curfew. They would set their own time to be home. Each of my kids turned eighteen the summer before their senior year of high school. Both of my kids went through their senior year without a curfew.

Now, this didn't happen overnight. I started early on: When they left the house they were expected to be home at a certain time. When they started dating, they had curfews. If they missed the curfew, they knew what the consequence was.

When they no longer had a curfew, they still had to tell me about what time they would be home, where they were going, and with whom they were going. This is just common courtesy for everyone in the family. One Friday night my son called at about

I ALWAYS TOLD THEM WHERE I WOULD BE and approximately what time I'd be home. If you want your kids to respect you, then you have to model that by respecting them.

eleven o'clock to tell me his friend had fixed him up with a blind date and they had taken the girls home. The girls lived on the opposite side of town from where we lived.

About midnight, the friend's mom called me in a panic because she didn't know where her son was, except that he was with Brian. I told her about the phone call, and then I said, "I know my son, and he is directionally challenged, and I imagine they got on the turnpike going the wrong direction. I figure it's going to be around two before they get home." We had a good laugh. A little after two she called back in a panic. As I was calming her down, her son came home. In a few minutes I heard my son's car pull into the driveway.

"Mom, are you okay? Why are you still up?" I said, "Son, I was worried about you. What happened?" Sure enough, they had gone the wrong way on the turnpike, gotten lost, and finally found their way home. I told him I was tired and we'd talk about his consequence in the morning. He questioned, "Consequence? But, Mom, I called you to tell you I was going to be late." I said, "Yes, you did, and I appreciate that. But I stayed up waiting for you because I was worried about you. I know how you are with directions. And now I'm going to be very tired all day in the meetings I have. What could you have done to avoid this?" He decided he should have planned ahead and figured out where they were going and how to get back home. (We didn't have iPhones back then.)

The next day I gave him a choice of consequences. He could be grounded for two weeks, or he could do forty hours of community service in my child care center. He chose the community service.

Parenting Forward

I began to look at parenting as a journey that I was traveling. At first it seemed like parenting would last forever. That's all I would ever be or do—I would just be a parent. When my daughter was fifteen, I thought that year would never end. It would just go on and on and on. My other thought was that she might not make it to her sixteenth birthday. Do you have days like that?

This parenting journey we are on does reach its destination. The destination is when your child becomes an adult. Sometimes the road just seems to inch by, and other times we travel at the speed of light.

Parenting our kids is a temporary job, not an identity. One time I had a lady in one of my administrative classes I was teaching who had ten children. And she was a single parent. She said that from the time her first child was born until the time her last child became an adult would be thirty-eight years. And yet, if she lives to be seventy-five or eighty, which is very possible, only half of her life will have been spent parenting children.

Making Your Job Easier

After my divorce from my children's dad I went to a very wise and older counselor at the Boston Methodist Church in Tulsa, Oklahoma. This man gave me some tremendous parenting advice. He said to think about rules and consequences in three different parts.

First are suggestions. Suggestions are one-way propositions. The parent suggests something, and it's up to the child to accept or neglect the suggestion. When my son was eleven, these were some of my suggestions:

1. Wash your face, arms, and hands each morning.
2. Brush your teeth each morning and evening.
3. Do homework before using any electronics, including watching TV.

4. Put your bike in the garage every evening.

5. Empty the downstairs trash.

Second are bargains—these are two-way propositions. The parent makes a statement, and the child can agree with a bargain, or the child can come back with a proposition. Discussion is part of bargaining. Here are a couple of the bargains my son and I made:

1. Keep your room clean and straightened up daily. If you can do this during the week, then on Saturday mornings when you are home, you can watch cartoons and any other appropriate TV shows you like.

2. If you can feed the dog and give her water at least once a day, then we can keep the dog and she can sleep in your room.

Third are the rules with consequences—these are not up for debate. These are set by the parent. Here are a few rules with consequences I had for my eleven-year-old son:

1. If you play music after nine in the evening, then it will be removed from your room for one week.

2. Lay out your clothes for school the night before. If you have problems finding things in the morning, then you will go to bed an hour early that night.

3. If you leave your things out downstairs at night, then I will get you up when I wake at five in the morning to pick everything up.

A suggestion can move to the bargaining place, and a bargain can be moved to the rules with consequences category when and if needed. I wrote everything out, and we discussed all of it. Then I asked, "Is there anything about this you don't understand?" Then I had them sign it. There was never any, "Well, I didn't know that was the rule." Or "I didn't understand what you meant."

I had very few rules with consequences. After a few years when my son became a teen, it wasn't necessary to put things in writing. We talked and bargained. (By the way, this kid was great in debate club at school.)

Good Communication

"A word fitly spoken is like apples of gold in a setting of silver" (Proverbs 25:11 NRSV).

Good discipline means good communication with your children. Realize that in the area of communication skills, it is normally the parent who makes the mistakes.

Are you guilty of any of the following?

- Assuming children understand your expectations.
- Not expressing what you expect in positive terms.
- Competing with other distractions.
- Asking incriminating questions. Never ask a child a question to which you already know the answer. For example, you saw your eight-year-old hit the six-year-old, and you ask, "Did you hit your sister?" The child is almost always going to say, "No!" Then what do you do? It would be better to say, "Jamie, I saw you hit your sister just now. In our family we are helpful people, and we are kind to each other. What could you have done instead of hitting her?"
- Not acknowledging children's feelings.
- Judging or criticizing feelings. They are the children's feelings, and they have a right to them.

Consequences

"For even when we were with you, we gave you this rule: 'If a man will not work, he shall not eat'" (2 Thessalonians 3:10). This was a favorite Scripture from the time my kids were in elementary school and all through high school. I quoted it often. This is a good example of a consequence: You don't work—you don't eat! Or you don't eat with the family, anyway.

Consequences can be natural or logical. A natural consequence is what happens naturally as a result of certain choices or behaviors. A logical consequence is a consequence that is set by the adult when a natural consequence would be unsafe.

An example of a natural consequence is when a child goes to school and doesn't eat breakfast. About midmorning he is going to be hungry.

An example of using a logical consequence: "If you are grouchy in the morning because you chose to stay up too late, then you will go to bed an hour earlier tomorrow night."

Logical consequences

- relate to the behavior,
- are respectful to both the child and the adult,
- are reasonable to both parties, and
- allow children to maintain their dignity.

Natural consequences should not be used when

- there is immediate danger to the child,
- there is immediate danger to another person,
- future consequences are at stake (brushing teeth, for example), or
- a child is not old enough to understand.

Use the following statement and put it in writing for your child: "If you do _____ then _____ will happen."

Always remember that you are the adult. You are the shepherd, and children need to be reassured that you are in control and that you are providing a safe environment for them. A parent who is in control or in charge actually empowers the child.

Empowerment means you

- encourage children to think for themselves,
- help them make wise decisions and choices,
- allow them to become responsible for their own actions, and
- don't rescue. For example, your middle school kid forgets her band instrument. She texts and asks you to bring it to her. If you do, that is rescuing your child.

Children will take power over their lives if you don't allow them some power over it themselves.

- Preschoolers will do it through not eating or not becoming toilet trained.
- Elementary children will do it by acting out in class or not doing their homework.
- Adolescents will do it through ditching school, running away, joining a gang or choosing inappropriate friends, engaging in sexual activities, or using drugs or alcohol.

Children associate good, effective discipline with love. The sheep follow the shepherd who protects and guides them, who cares for them and keeps them out of harm's way.

Can we not do that for our own children?

Can we do any less than be their shepherd?

"My sheep hear my voice, and I know them, and they follow me" (John 10:27 ESV).

There is so much to talk about when discussing behavior and discipline. Throughout this book, you'll find many examples of and guidance for disciplining children. This chapter has only hit the highlights.

GOING DEEPER

1. Psalm 23 can lend comfort to our hectic lives as single parents. What goes through your mind when you think about

   • the peace of lying in green pastures?
   • the comfort of God being over us, in charge of us?
   • the security of God as our own Shepherd?
   • the Lord guiding us in right paths and right ways?
   • God meeting all of our needs (i.e., food in the presence of enemies)?

2. Think of a successful single parent you know. What makes him or her successful? List all of these things. Which of these can you replicate in your family?

3. Regarding learning styles:
   Your learning style is _____.
   Your children's learning styles are _____
   _____.

   How will knowing your learning style and those of your children help you in parenting? _____
   _____
   _____

4. When your children are adults, what character traits and qualities do you want them to possess?
   1. _____
   2. _____
   3. _____
   4. _____
   5. _____
   6. _____

4

Supporting Your Children When You Have Them Part Time

A Father's Plea

While this chapter deals mainly with the parent who doesn't have custodial care, custodial parents can learn from this chapter also. Sometimes custodial parents must learn to accept the reality that there is another parent in their children's lives. Whether you have sole custody or shared parenting, you've been deserted, or your child's other parent has died, there is always something to be gleaned from Scripture.

Dwayne[1] is an incredible father to his kids, even though they live quite a distance from him. He supports his children financially. He supports them emotionally. He has a good relationship with each of his children, some of whom are now adults. He prays for his kids and asks others to pray for them.

When Dwayne was married he was in the military and had to be away from his family several times for extended periods. After spending a year away from home on assignment overseas, he came home to a fractured family. Even though he had kept in touch with his wife and kids on an almost daily basis, his marriage was unraveling. He admits he didn't have God in his life and says, "Without God in our relationship, it was doomed."

Right after the separation, Dwayne's wife lived just down the street from him. The kids could come and go at each house. This gave Dad an opportunity to influence his kids in life skills such as how to spend and save money. He went on humorous outings with his kids. He shared in our DivorceCare[2] group how he talked to his kids about bullies and not being a bully, and about how to have friends and enjoy life. This was a great time for him and the kids.

After the divorce was final, the mother of his kids moved eight hours away. There wasn't anything he could do about it. Dwayne joined our group at church after his ex-wife and kids had moved out of town. He was hungry to know more about the Lord, and he was lonely and missing his kids.

Dwayne impressed all of us in our DivorceCare group because of his tender attitude toward his kids and their mother. He didn't harbor any ill will toward her, which was amazing because she almost bankrupted him. She had done a lot of financial damage while he was away serving our country for a year. Eventually he had to send her to a rehab facility. She had destroyed the family, and yet this tenderhearted man bore no animosity toward her.

Since he was still in the military, he couldn't just pack up and follow the kids to another location. He stays in contact with his kids by phone. When they were younger, his children came every summer to spend time with him. All the kids came every other Christmas until the older kids got jobs of their own.

I'll never forget the summer his daughter received the Lord Jesus Christ as her personal Savior. We had prayed for this child, and we rejoiced with this father that her belief in God and Christ was solid. We rejoiced with him when she was baptized at the end of vacation Bible school at our church.

Noncustodial Parents Can Still Influence Their Children

Many noncustodial parents feel left out of their children's lives because they don't live with them on a daily basis. It might be difficult for the noncustodial parent or the parent in a shared parenting situation to take an active role in the spiritual development of their children. Perhaps you are one of those parents. Whether your children live with you or not, it is your responsibility to impact their spiritual development. It may mean you get creative in pouring God's truth into them. If your former spouse forbids you to have contact or talk about spiritual things, it is still your responsibility to pray for them on a daily basis.

Many dads have shared that they think it is their responsibility. Dwayne prayed fervently for all of his children. He lives a Christian life by studying God's Word and leading a Bible study class at church.

Another dad, Barry Cummings, feels it is his responsibility to impact his daughter's life by how he lives his life for the Lord. Below he shares his story and what he did to help himself move forward.

The moment I realized that I would not have my daughter with me every day was gut-wrenching. Soon after my separation I noticed a family making a custody exchange at a gas station, and it hit me hard. How would I stay connected during her away time when she was with her mom?

The first thing I could think of was to pray to my heavenly Father for guidance because He is the only one who has complete control over anything. Second, I was going to have to take the high road for my child's sake and get along with my soon-to-be-ex. Third, being a child of divorce myself, I knew what not to do because of the mistakes my parents made with me. I immediately got involved with a DivorceCare group in my area to get help and encouragement to recover from my divorce.

78

My daughter was two years old when her mom and I divorced. I have been a Christian since 2001, and even before my daughter was born I prayed that she would be saved and follow the Lord. As she has grown up, I have tried to show her what a relationship with the Lord looks like. For me, I start my morning off with prayer time, devotional reading and Bible study. I wanted Tara to see her dad make our heavenly Father a priority. I found out that Tara really did pay attention to my actions.

Saturday mornings in the fall are exciting in Alabama, as we love our Crimson Tide football team. One Saturday there was an early kickoff at 11:00 a.m. As with most Bama games, I was having some folks over for it. As it would happen, Tara and I slept late that morning, and in a rush to get everything ready for our company, I skipped my devotion time. At the end of the evening, my beautiful six-year-old daughter asked me a tough question, "Daddy, why didn't you read your Bible this morning?"

That cut me to my core. She was paying attention and taking it all in—the good and the bad. I had to apologize to my daughter and let her know that my priorities were wrong that day.

On Father's Day, 2013, my sweet Tara walked the aisle and gave her life to Christ.

From a Distance or Nearby, Dads Have a Responsibility

These are only two of the men I know personally who believe it is important to impact their children's lives for the Lord. Dwayne does it from a distance and Barry on a regular visitation schedule.

Another story a young friend shared with me is quite sad. She shared it as a prayer request for her friend, a young teen whose dad had remarried. After she felt like she was being forgotten, her dad invited her to go on a trip with him and his new wife. She was so excited and told all of her friends about it. Then he said, "You'll have to earn your own money to pay for the trip."

While she was a little upset she'd have to pay for it, she was still excited to think her dad wanted her on this trip, until he said, "I had my stepkids pay their own way, so you'll have to do it too." She said, "Wait! You took your stepkids on a trip before you took your own daughter?"

She was livid to say the least. She loudly declined the opportunity to go on the trip. Can you blame her? My young friend was very concerned about the girl's welfare, and we prayed for her often. I don't know what happened to this young teen, but I'd venture to say that she does not have a relationship with her father. This dad did not take his responsibility seriously.

A Single Parent in the Bible?

Let's look at one man in the Bible who had to send his child to live with the child's mother quite a distance away.

In Genesis chapter 16 we learn about Abram's wife, Sarai, and her Egyptian maid, Hagar. When I first read about and studied Hagar, her story was uplifting to me because Hagar is actually the first single parent in the Bible. Not only was she the first single parent, she was also what might be called in today's vernacular a surrogate parent.

Hagar caught my attention because when I first became a single parent, I felt more or less useless in the Christian realm. I felt I had failed God because, after all, He hates divorce. As it says in Malachi 2:16, "'I hate divorce,' says the Lord God of Israel."

Because God hates divorce, I thought I didn't fit in at church any more. Or maybe the church I attended didn't accept me very well as a single, divorced parent. But when I read about Hagar I started thinking, "Hey, if a single parent is talked about in the Bible, maybe, just maybe, I'm going to be okay." I knew that God loved me and would never desert me, but still it helped tremendously to read about a single parent in the Old Testament.

Let's Look More Closely at This Story in the Bible

Now Sarai, Abram's wife, had borne him no children. But she had an Egyptian maidservant named Hagar; so she said to Abram, "The Lord has kept me from having children. Go, sleep with my maidservant; perhaps I can build a family through her." Abram agreed to what Sarai said. So after Abram had been living in Canaan ten years, Sarai his wife took her Egyptian maidservant Hagar and gave her to her husband to be his wife. He slept with Hagar, and she conceived. When she knew she was pregnant, she began to despise her mistress.

Genesis 16:1–4

In order to fully understand where God is coming from in this story with Abram and his firstborn son, go back and read the entire sixteenth chapter of Genesis. As you read, you'll see that Sarai took matters into her own hands. It wasn't God's design that Hagar give Abram children. It was Sarai's idea. But then in 16:5 we read, "Then Sarai said to Abram, 'You are responsible for the wrong I am suffering. I put my servant in your arms, and now that she knows she is pregnant, she despises me.'"

We always pay a price when we don't follow God's design for our lives. Sarai was paying this price when her maid began to despise her. Sometimes, however, as in Hagar's situation, it is not our choice. Hagar was given to Abram by Sarai, and even if she didn't want to be the surrogate parent, it wasn't up to her. Some of us didn't want to be a single parent either, but because of another person's doing, this is where we ended up. We will talk more about Hagar in chapter 12, but for now, let's concentrate on Abram and Ishmael.

"So Hagar bore Abram a son, and Abram gave the name Ishmael to the son she had borne. Abram was eighty-six years old when Hagar bore him Ishmael" (Genesis 16:15–16).

What do we learn about Ishmael from this passage?

- Ishmael was Abram's only son for almost fourteen years.
- We can conclude that Ishmael's dad must have loved him very much.

81

• Even though Ishmael was Abram's only son, this was not God's original plan for Abram.

God allowed Ishmael to be born, but He had other, bigger plans for Abram. Later, in the seventeenth chapter of Genesis, God lays out His plan. Abram walked faithfully and blamelessly before the Lord. When Abram was ninety-nine years old the Lord appeared before him. This is when the Lord told him He would make a covenant with Abram and make him the father of many nations.

Abram fell facedown, and God said to him, "As for me, this is my covenant with you: You will be the father of many nations. No longer will you be called Abram; your name will be Abraham, for I have made you a father of many nations. I will make you very fruitful; I will make nations of you, and kings will come from you. I will establish my covenant as an everlasting covenant between me and you and your descendants after you for the generations to come, to be your God and the God of your descendants after you."

Genesis 17:3–7

God goes on to explain in Genesis 17:15–16 that Sarai, who will now be called Sarah, will be the mother of this new nation.

Imagine the confusion a ninety-nine-year-old man must have felt. All these years his wife had been barren. He has a thirteen-year-old son by his wife's maidservant, and now God is telling him that his ninety-year-old wife is finally going to conceive a son? Abraham fell facedown and laughed (v. 17).

Then Abraham Remembers His Son, Ishmael

Abraham then becomes concerned about his only son to date, Ishmael. Abraham could have just written Ishmael off. He could have thought that now with his wife having a child, Hagar and Ishmael could move along. But Abraham doesn't forget about Ishmael.

Abraham asks God to bless his son. Have you asked God to bless your children?

What exactly does it mean to "bless" a child? For our purposes in this lesson, let's use the idea of watching closely over somebody and declaring approval and support for someone.

> And Abraham said to God, "If only Ishmael might live under your blessing!" Then God said, "Yes, but your wife Sarah will bear you a son, and you will call him Isaac. I will establish my covenant with him as an everlasting covenant for his descendants after him. And as for Ishmael, I have heard you: I will surely bless him; I will make him fruitful and will greatly increase his numbers. He will be the father of twelve rulers, and I will make him into a great nation."
>
> Genesis 17:18–20

Abraham, the father of Ishmael, asks for blessings for his son. He is promised so much from God, but he still asks that God bless Ishmael. In our day and age, this father's plea to God for his son should be an example for fathers the world over.

Many people don't know what to ask for when bestowing a blessing upon their child. When I was with a group of single parents, I asked them how they thought single dads could bless their children today. Here is the list they shared:

- Send handwritten and signed notes and cards through the mail.
- Text or FaceTime your kids when you know they have a test or some event coming up that day. Tell the child you are praying for him or her.
- Remember special days—maybe a sporting event or a concert at school.
- Send special books and write short messages in them for your kid.
- Follow through; don't leave the child hanging and wondering if or when you are going to show up.

- Don't make empty promises.
- Do not forget the child's birthday—ever!
- Tell your children often that God loves them.

I'm sure you can come up with more ideas of ways to bless your children.

Think about it: God had just told Abraham that he was going to be the father of many nations, but Abraham takes the time to ask, "But what about Ishmael—can't you bless him?" In other words, Abraham remembers his son. What an awesome testimony to a father's love. He could very well have just forgotten all about Ishmael and gone on with his life.

In today's world, many fathers (and mothers also) seem to forget about their children when they remarry, get a big promotion at work, or move across the country with a new spouse. What if Abraham lived in our world today? Do you think he still would have remembered his son by the surrogate?

One Dad's Story of Remembering His Child

Many fathers who don't live with their children still take their role seriously. Here is one personal testimony of Jackson Hardy, a father who works at being the spiritual leader for a child he has to share with a person in another home.

As a single father, I am reminded in Deuteronomy that I am to teach my children to hear God's words and learn to revere God and follow all His commandments all their lives and teach them to their children.

And these words which I command you this day shall be upon your heart; and you shall teach them diligently to your children, and shall talk of them when you sit in your house, and when you walk by the way, and when you lie down, and when you rise.

Deuteronomy 6:6–7 RSV

I think that as a single Christian father, the most important job I have is still being the spiritual head of my household, and I am commanded to bring the Word into my children's lives. If I fail at this command, I remember the passage in Exodus 34:6b–7:

The LORD God, merciful and gracious, longsuffering, and abundant in goodness and truth, keeping mercy for thousands, forgiving iniquity and transgression and sin, and that will by no means clear the guilty; visiting the iniquity of the fathers upon the children, and upon the children's children, unto the third and to the fourth generation.

Exodus 34:6–7 KJV

Who would want to bring that burden to their family's future generations?

Just as the Lord expects me to abide by my covenant with Him, I have a responsibility to society to provide care, food, clothes, and shelter for my offspring.

Parental Conflict[3]

Instead of putting kids first and trying to bless their children, a lot of fathers and mothers get wrapped up in custody disputes, mediation, and court battles, where the child pays a big price for the discord.

Many things affect children when parents divorce. However, there is one big, overwhelming variable that causes kids of divorce angst and anxiety—and that is when parents continue to war with each other. Parental conflict affects children for many years to come.

When parents continue to fight, that does several things to the children in the family.

- Often kids are drawn into the battle. The lines are drawn by the warring parents, and the kids feel like they must take sides. This is very unfair to young kids.

85

- Other times, children withdraw completely. They fear they will have to take sides, so they withdraw into themselves. These kids can experience overwhelming depression.
- Some children wonder if they will ever be able to trust adults again. After all, if the adults they love the most are acting this way, how do other adults act when they are upset? Remember, the kids have only known these adults as their parents. They didn't know these two people before they were parents.
- Kids wonder, "Does love ever last? I thought my parents loved each other, but look at how they are acting toward each other now."
- Some kids wonder, "Since my parents quit loving each other and are acting so ridiculous, will they quit loving me and act like that toward me?"
- Some kids grieve the loss of the intact family. They grieve alone and deal with the pain alone.

Some research shows that children as young as six months can be affected by parental conflict. Babies sense something is wrong. Loud and angry voices can be scary. The infant can feel the emotions of the parents. The baby or toddler cries out of fear, and this upsets the parents even more, leading to a vicious circle where sleep and calm routines are affected by the stress of the parents fighting.

Children and teens have shared with me they have experienced parents exhibiting the following during conflict:

- screaming at the top of their lungs
- lacking regard or respect for each other
- deep, scary growling, usually from the dad
- slamming fists into walls and cars
- name-calling
- threatening to ruin the other parent's reputation on social media

- never-ending arguing—every time the parents see each other, the same argument ensues
- screaming while the other parent walks away
- using the silent treatment to get what they want from the other parent and then laughing about it later

Do you think these kids are learning to problem solve? More than likely they will only repeat what they see their parents do.

The Fatherless Generation

I realize that not all noncustodial parents are fathers, but since most are, I think it's important to talk about the huge issue of fatherlessness in our country today. Our society is suffering from a fatherless generation. When we look at the most troubled segments of our young population—suicides, runaways, dropouts, etc.—some legacies of children raised without fathers directly involved are clear.

- 63 percent of teens who commit suicide come from fatherless homes.
- 90 percent of all runaways and homeless children are from fatherless homes.
- 71 percent of all kids who drop out of high school come from fatherless homes.
- 75 percent of all adolescents in substance abuse centers come from fatherless homes.
- 85 percent of all juveniles in prison come from fatherless homes.
- Daughters who don't have involved fathers are 164 percent more likely to have a premarital birth.[4]

In Kathy Rodriguez's book *Healing the Father Wound* we read, "We as a society reap the consequences of a fatherless generation whether we like it or not. The woundedness is there all around us and in us. If we are to prevent the effects of fatherlessness from spilling to the next generation, healing in our nation must bind up the brokenhearted who suffer from father woundedness, and also provide men with powerful hands-on guidance in effective fathering."[5]

We don't have to be this wounded in our world today. Not all children raised in fatherless homes experience the legacies listed above. There are many fathers who do take responsibility for their children and stay connected to their children after a divorce. However, there are many more fathers who do not take responsibility, or take very little. Research is showing that fathers who cohabitate with a child's mother are less likely to stick around as the child grows. It appears, as one minister said, we have fathers with hard hearts.

Abraham is a good example of a father who provided for his son when his son had to be sent away. It appears Abraham had a soft and caring heart for Ishmael. After Sarah gave birth to Isaac, she got very jealous of Ishmael and requested that Abraham send Ishmael and Hagar away.

"The child grew and was weaned, and on the day Isaac was weaned Abraham held a great feast. But Sarah saw that the son whom Hagar the Egyptian had borne to Abraham was mocking, and she said to Abraham, 'Get rid of that slave woman and her son, for that slave woman's son will never share in the inheritance with my son Isaac'" (Genesis 21:8–10).

What do you think Abraham thought about this demand? And what would you have done if you had been Abraham?

The matter distressed Abraham greatly because it concerned his son. But God said to him, "Do not be so distressed about the boy and your maidservant. Listen to whatever Sarah tells you, because it is through Isaac that your offspring will be reckoned. I will make the son of the maidservant into a nation also, because he is your offspring." Early the next morning Abraham took some food and a skin of water and gave them to Hagar. He set them on her shoulders and then sent her off with the boy. She went on her way and wandered in the desert of Beersheba.

Genesis 21:11–14

For Noncustodial Parents

As a noncustodial parent, you may sometimes be confused about what your role is. Be aware that you still have a strong influence on your children, regardless of how often you see them. While it's not easy, other noncustodial parents have done it. Your children are very aware of your actions and decisions regarding their lives, and they know if you pray for them. Be involved, and consistently reassure them of your love, not only with your words but also with your actions.

As for Ishmael, God did provide for and take care of him. When Ishmael and Hagar were traveling to be with her people, they got lost in the desert of Beersheba. They lay down to die, but God heard their cries and provided a well of water, and He must have provided safety for them as they traveled.

"God was with the boy as he grew up. He lived in the desert and became an archer. While he was living in the Desert of Paran, his mother got a wife for him from Egypt" (Genesis 21:20–21).

We can assume from reading Genesis 25 that Ishmael must have maintained a relationship with his father. At Abraham's death Ishmael was there with his brother Isaac to bury his father. "Then Abraham breathed his last and died at a good old age, an old man and full of years; and he was gathered to his people. His sons Isaac and Ishmael buried him in the cave of Machpelah near Mamre, in the field of Ephron son of Zohar the Hittite" (Genesis 25:8–9).

As you read more about Ishmael in Genesis 25:12–18, you will see that he lived a long life and was blessed with twelve sons. "These were the sons of Ishmael, and these are the names of the twelve tribal rulers according to their settlements and camps.

Altogether, Ishmael lived a hundred and thirty-seven years. He breathed his last and died, and he was gathered to his people" (Genesis 25:16–17).

If you are a noncustodial parent, spend time this week in prayer seeking out what the Lord expects and wants of you regarding the children who do not live with you.

If you know noncustodial parents, pray for them this week. Pray for their comfort and for their relationship with their children. You might try giving them a call to encourage them and share some of the concepts in this lesson.

"Sons are a heritage from the Lord, children a reward from him. Like arrows in the hands of a warrior are sons born in one's youth. Blessed is the man whose quiver is full of them. They will not be put to shame when they contend with their enemies in the gate" (Psalm 127:3–5).

Warning: Do not use this chapter to beat your ex over the head!!!

GOING DEEPER

1. What are some problems our society is creating because many feel entitled to usurp God's plan?

2. In what way was the family that Sarai wanted to start different from surrogate families today?

3. What are some ways fathers who do not live with their children can bless their children?

4. What are some ways that mothers can encourage and support the role of the father in their child's life?

5. What about children who have no father in their lives? What are some things the mother (or guardian) can do to bring Christian male figures into a child's life?

6. Why do some children from fatherless homes experience the horrific outcomes mentioned earlier but others don't?

7. Abraham took his role as Ishmael's father very seriously. If fathers today followed Abraham's example, what would be some things they (you) would need to do to provide for their children when they don't live with them?

5

Learning to Accept Other People into Your Child's Life

Two Mothers—One Son

One day my friend Kim told me her story, and I knew immediately it fit this chapter. While all single parents' stories are different, each story has something in common—either there is a hurting child or there is a hurting parent. Kim is a hurting parent.

Kim's ex-husband lived far away, and per their agreement she had to travel across the country to take her daughter to stay with Dad for the summer. Mom had entertained the thought that they might get back together since they had been talking about the possibility of reconciling. When she got there, she realized he didn't love her. He continued having affairs, and Kim decided she couldn't go back into that marriage. She left her daughter for the summer as planned.

By the time summer was over, he had remarried, was being transferred out of the country, and was taking their daughter with him. He had money and could purchase just about anything his daughter desired. Kim didn't have the funds to purchase a lot of things for her daughter, but she did, however, provide a good home for her—it just wasn't full of all the expensive electronics the daughter wanted. Plus, it sounded exciting to this teenage girl to go live in another country. Kim said she knew her daughter would be safe with her father and that he would meet all of her financial needs.

When Kim returned home at the beginning of summer she found out she had cancer. She didn't have the funds to fight for custody of her daughter, and since she was being treated with chemo, she didn't have the energy to fight either. She was very sick all summer, and when her ex moved overseas, she lost contact with him and her daughter.

Through some maneuvering and searching, she finally found her ex-husband, but according to him their daughter now refused to talk to Kim and refused to come home. Kim never told her daughter about the cancer because she knew her ex-husband would say she was making it all up to get their daughter to move back to the States. As of the writing of this book, Kim has not talked to or heard from her daughter. It is a sad situation for my friend.

She is not the only parent who has lost a child. It happens many more times than we like to think. Sometimes as the result of a judge's proclamation awarding a child to the other parent, and at other times, as in Kim's situation, the other parent disappears with the child.

Baby Moses

If you went to church at all as a child, you probably heard the story of baby Moses being put in a basket and floated down the river. A princess finds the baby and takes him in as her own. As a child, I couldn't figure out why a mother would put her baby in a basket and float him down the river alone, but as an adult after my divorce, I came to realize what a powerful story this is in so many ways.

First, we learn God had special plans for Moses' life. God was in control the entire time. But the story also jumped out at me as a single mom. I began to realize through this story that my children were going to have a life that had nothing to do with me. They were going to meet people who would influence them whom I didn't know. When my ex-husband remarried, I didn't know his new wife. While I might have wanted to sit and chat with her about the kids, that opportunity was never afforded me.

My kids seemed to like their dad's new wife. They talked about her favorably. They went to see their dad every other weekend, and she was always there. As they became older teens, because of jobs and school they didn't visit their dad as much, but I finally got to meet his wife at my son's college graduation. The funny thing is my kids never considered this lady to be their stepmom. She was just a lady in their dad's life, but she was still a part of their life that didn't include me. For us moms, that is quite difficult to accept.

Two Mothers and One Son in the Bible

You may remember from the first chapter of Exodus that Pharaoh had issued orders for all the Hebrew babies to be killed. For a more in-depth understanding, read the entire first chapter of Exodus, but we will pick up the story here:

> Now a man of the house of Levi married a Levite woman, and she became pregnant and gave birth to a son. When she saw that he was a fine child, she hid him for three months. But when she could hide him no longer, she got a papyrus basket for him and coated it with tar and pitch. Then she placed the child in it and put it among the reeds along the bank of the Nile. His sister stood at a distance to see what would happen to him.
>
> Then Pharaoh's daughter went down to the Nile to bathe, and her attendants were walking along the river bank. She saw the basket among the reeds and sent her slave girl to get it. She opened it

and saw the baby. He was crying, and she felt sorry for him. "This is one of the Hebrew babies," she said.

Exodus 2:1–6

Pharaoh's daughter knew this was a Hebrew baby, the very nationality and age group her father, the Pharaoh, had ordered killed, and yet she felt sorrow for this infant. She could have adopted a baby from her people, but she was drawn to this Hebrew baby.

What do you think went through the mind of Moses' birth mother when she knew there was no way to get around Pharaoh's command?

We can only imagine what she thought when her beautiful baby boy was born. How on earth did she hatch this plan to float her baby down the river Nile? Do you think maybe God planted that in her mind? I believe He did, just like the Holy Spirit plants thoughts in our minds today regarding our children.

This mom kept her baby hidden for months, and then she did what she thought was best for him. She was taking a big risk putting her baby in a basket and floating him on the Nile River—the basket could have turned over, drowning her baby, or soldiers could have found the baby and killed him. She was a desperate mother who loved her baby so much she was willing to do whatever it took to save his life.

In our world today, we have desperate moms. Some are

- single by choice,
- never married,
- divorced,
- widowed,
- mothers who adopted a child,
- stepmothers, or
- foster mothers.

But they all are moms who want to protect and care for their children. Many will take desperate measures to protect them. Moses' mom had to find a way to protect her baby and shield him from death.

While most moms today are not in that dire a situation, they do want to shield their children or limit exposure to unsavory people such as a parent who has been incarcerated or a parent with drug or alcohol addictions, but because of custody arrangements their hands are tied, and they have no choice but to send their children to the other home. Some moms who have to share their children with the other parent can't protect the children when they are at the other home.[1]

As we continue to read the story, we find that Miriam, Moses' sister, stood by and kept a close eye on her baby brother.

When Pharaoh's daughter opened the basket, she cared about the baby. She could just as well have called the soldiers or even the Pharaoh himself to deal with the baby, but she didn't. God had plans for Moses.

What can we learn by reading this passage about Moses?

- God wanted the Egyptian princess to find the baby.
- God wanted Moses to be raised by her so he would be educated and respected as a son of the Pharaoh and trained in the way of the king's people.
- God wanted Moses' life saved.
- God wanted to use Moses to deliver the children of Israel to the Promised Land.

God has plans for your children just as He did for Moses. It might not seem like it, or even appear that God remembers your children, but don't usurp God's authority in your life and in your children's lives by making your children follow your dreams. You don't know what is in store for your children ten, fifteen, or even twenty years down the line.

Do you think Moses' birth mother, the Levite woman, knew what was going to happen to her son? I doubt it.

As we read the story we see that Miriam suggested to Pharaoh's daughter that she go and find a woman to nurse him. Of course, we know that this "nurse" she was going to find was Moses' birth mother.

> Then his sister asked Pharaoh's daughter, "Shall I go and get one of the Hebrew women to nurse the baby for you?"
> "Yes, go," she answered. And the girl went and got the baby's mother. Pharaoh's daughter said to her, "Take this baby and nurse him for me, and I will pay you." So the woman took the baby and nursed him. When the child grew older, she took him to Pharaoh's daughter and he became her son. She named him Moses, saying, "I drew him out of the water."
>
> Exodus 2:7–10

Isn't it interesting that the princess names her child "I drew him out of the water," and years later water would play an important role in the children of Israel leaving Egypt? The Lord would use Moses to turn the water into blood to help convince Pharaoh to let the people go. Then the Lord would use Moses to take the children of Israel across the Red Sea, their escape from Pharaoh.

We don't know anything about the period when the baby lived with his birth mother. However, we can draw some conclusions.

- We do know that his birth mother loved him enough to give him to the Egyptian princess. She handed over this baby she carried and birthed and nursed to another mother.
- The birth mother knew that her son was going to have a different lifestyle, very different from her other children's.
- She understood that her son was going to worship pagan gods and worship like the Egyptian royalty.
- Perhaps she thought she would have enough influence over his life that she could circumvent what he would

experience in the Egyptian household. Or perhaps she trusted God enough to let go, knowing God would protect and provide.

I imagine she prayed for her son continuously. As was the custom then, she might have even offered sacrifices in worship to God. What lessons can we take from this Levite mother?

• Trust God.
• Do not question God's authority in your life, but accept with faith His plans.
• Pray for your children without ceasing.
• Never forget your children, even if they are taken from you.
• Remember that you have a terrific influence over your children.

We now know from brain research that babies hear when they are in the womb. Babies connect with the mother right after birth, and while they might not remember these things, we know that memories from before the child can speak are kept and stored in the brain. If young babies are neglected, are not fed, don't get their diapers changed, etc., that can affect them the rest of their lives. Children must attach to a primary caregiver. While we don't know for sure, it is likely that, as is typical with newborns, baby Moses connected with his mother when she nursed him before she put him in the Nile River. More than likely he continued growing in his attachment to her after the Egyptian princess asked the mother to nurse Moses for her.

The life of Moses and his relationship with his adopted mother, the Pharaoh's daughter, and with his birth mother, is a good example of how mothers who have to share their children with another woman can survive.

This lesson in the Bible accentuates the feelings many of today's parents experience when a stepparent or girlfriend (or boyfriend) enters the picture.

We can't know for sure the interactions of the two women in Moses' life. But the Egyptian mother must have allowed Moses to know his Hebrew heritage and roots because when Moses grew up he knew he was of Hebrew heritage.

> One day, after Moses had grown up, he went out to where his own people were and watched them at their hard labor. He saw an Egyptian beating a Hebrew, one of his own people. Glancing this way and that and seeing no one, he killed the Egyptian and hid him in the sand.
>
> Exodus 2:11–12

I doubt the Levite mother had much say in what happened to her son. Today's single parents need to realize they can't control what goes on in the other home. You can't control your adult children either, and by the time your child is fifteen or sixteen, your role becomes one of coach and influencer. Your parenting and instilling of morals, biblical truths, etc. should be done when they are younger.

Think Ahead about What You Can't Control

As a single parent, you need to know how you are going to handle different situations that your child might come home and report. There are some things you will not be able to control.

For example, what are you going to do when your child tells you he met Dad's or Mom's new friend?

When my kids came home all excited one Sunday evening and told me they had helped their dad rearrange his apartment because his girlfriend was moving in, I was devastated. I was still holding out hope we would reconcile. And to be truthful, it hurt that they were all excited and helpful in this situation. It only took me a short time to realize they were just happy for their dad and all caught up in his excitement.

I CALLED ALL OF OUR FRIENDS to find out what their rules were. I wanted to be fair to my daughter and not make our rules too strict. The other reason I called all of our friends to find out their rules was so that later on when she said, "Everyone's doing it!" I'd be able to pull out my list and say, "Uh, no, not the Robinsons or the Harmons," etc. This happened on several occasions. So, single mom or single dad, call your kids' friends' parents and find out what their rules are.

I had to get up extra early the next morning for a longer prayer time. I had to work through this new turn of events, and only the Lord could do that with me.

What about when your child reports something you don't approve of but that is not illegal, such as playing video games late into the night?

What about when you tell your child not to do something, but it's the other parent's weekend and he or she tells them yes?

When my daughter was turning fifteen, we sat down and made up our dating rules.

One of my rules was she couldn't date until she was fifteen and a half, and it had to be within a group. One day she came home and said, "Oh, Mom, I'm going to the fall dance with Trent."

I said, "What do you mean? You can't date until you're fifteen and a half, and that won't be until February." She replied, "Well, that's my dad's weekend, and there is nothing you can do about it. I asked him, and he told me I could go."

I learned early on that when things happened with my kids, I had to step back and take time to think about them. I didn't say anything to her then but just turned and walked away. I prayed about it. I thought about it. Then I went to her a few days later and said, "You are right—there is nothing I can do about this. However, you know I don't want you to do it. So after much prayer

I want you to know that I can't have any part of this. That means I won't buy you a dress or shoes or spend any money on this event because I don't approve of what you are doing."

Her Bible study teacher from church called me and told me I was being unreasonable and that she was going to give Julie a dress for this event. Our neighbor and church friend also thought I was being unreasonable, so she had the dress cleaned. Her dad's wife purchased some shoes, a purse, and a jacket.

On the weekend of the big dance, Julie and her friend got all of her stuff together, and when her dad came the two teens walked out the door giggling. I sat there alone all weekend wondering if I had done the right thing.

When she came home Sunday evening, I didn't ask about the dance. I didn't act mad or sullen. I was just myself. Life went on.

Years later, my daughter apologized and told me she didn't enjoy going to the dance at all. When I asked her why, she said, "Because I knew I had robbed you of seeing me go to my first dance. Didn't you notice that guy never asked me out again? I made him miserable too."

A Rift between Your Child and the Other Parent

How will you handle things when your child reports that they don't like going to the other home, and that they are not going to go back because the other parent has stepkids at their home?

When my friend Bobbi's son went to visit his dad and stepmom, he had no bedroom and no bed. The stepmom's twins had a bedroom and their own beds. The stepmom always treated him differently than her twins because she didn't like his mother. For years he spent every other weekend and summers at his dad's, and his father also treated him differently so as not to upset his wife. Bobbi didn't have a choice. All she could do was tell her son to talk to his dad about upcoming visits.

We can assume that Moses knew his birth mother, his sister, Miriam, and his brother, Aaron, because when God called Moses to lead His people out of Egypt, Moses complained that he couldn't speak well enough, and God sent his brother, Aaron, to speak for him.

> Moses said to the Lord, "O Lord, I have never been eloquent, neither in the past nor since you have spoken to your servant. I am slow of speech and tongue." . . .
> Then the Lord's anger burned against Moses and he said, "What about your brother, Aaron the Levite? I know he can speak well. He is already on his way to meet you, and his heart will be glad when he sees you."
>
> Exodus 4:10, 14

God meets all of our needs, even before we know what the need is. He will meet your children's needs also, if you allow it.

For Moses, God provided Miriam, the sister who watched Moses float down the Nile River and turned out to be a prophetess who led the people in singing when they were in the desert.

"Then Miriam the prophetess, Aaron's sister, took a tambourine in her hand, and all the women followed her, with tambourines and dancing" (Exodus 15:20).

Today Pharaoh's daughter could be called a "choice mom." She made a choice to take in baby Moses as her own son.

Today "choice moms" consist of many different types of mothers. Many choice moms, or SMCs (Single Mom by Choice), are women who, for whatever reasons, have not found a suitable husband or mate but want to have children. Maybe you are a single mom by choice.

- Some women are using artificial insemination to get pregnant.
- Some women adopt.
- Some women become SMCs because they are in the lesbian community.

We know from research that the outcomes for children raised by mothers alone and with no father in the picture are not as good as those for children in two-parent homes or in stepfamilies. In "The Science of Dad and the 'Father Effect'" we read, "Children with involved dads are less likely to break the law and drop out of school. Guided by close relationships with father figures, these kids disproportionately grow up to avoid risky sex, pursue healthy relationships, and hold down high-paying jobs."[2]

An article published by *Huffington Post* suggests, "Studies show that if your child's father is affectionate, supportive, and involved, he can contribute greatly to your child's cognitive, language, and social development, as well as academic achievement, a strong inner core resource, sense of well-being, good self-esteem, and authenticity."[3]

Many single moms raise healthy, functioning kids. Some do it by bringing in male mentors or strong Christian couples to influence their children. Others do it by depending on nearby relatives, such as grandparents, to advise them. Some single moms raise their kids to be successful by reading books on how to be a confident and successful single parent. For me it was depending upon the Lord and studying His Word when I was struggling with various situations. Many times, I would pray and then wait. I would wait for the Lord to speak to me or for myself to calm down so I could think logically. While it is difficult for single moms, and dads, to raise healthy, functioning kids, it is not impossible.

We don't know a lot about Moses' upbringing except that his adopted mother must have loved him very much. She also must have allowed him to know his Hebrew heritage because he knew his people were Hebrew. We don't know if Moses had any stepsiblings at his Egyptian home.

What we do know is that Moses was in God's hands. God had a plan for him, and He saw that His plan was executed. He did this by using the very people who wanted to kill all the Hebrew baby boys so the Hebrew nation couldn't survive and thrive—the Egyptians. And God used Pharaoh's own daughter to fulfill His plan.

Sometimes God uses the very people we might think are the enemy—the other woman, the other man, the foster parent, or the grandparent. Nothing is impossible with God. It might be hard to believe, but other people might be brought into your child's life who have nothing to do with you. We can pray God's intervention for every area of our children's lives.

"At that time Moses was born, and he was no ordinary child. For three months he was cared for by his family. When he was placed outside, Pharaoh's daughter took him and brought him up as her own son. Moses was educated in all the wisdom of the Egyptians and was powerful in speech and action" (Acts 7:20–22 NIV).

Moses did hear the Lord's call on his life. When he was called back to Egypt to rescue the Lord's people, he went. He led the people of Israel out of Egypt. We also know from reading Scripture that Moses rejected the earthly kingdom life of riches to live a life full of trials and tribulation for the Lord.

> By faith Moses, when he had grown up, refused to be known as the son of Pharaoh's daughter. He chose to be mistreated along with the people of God rather than to enjoy the fleeting pleasures of sin. He regarded disgrace for the sake of Christ as of greater value than the treasures of Egypt, because he was looking ahead to his reward. By faith he left Egypt, not fearing the king's anger; he persevered because he saw him who is invisible.
>
> Hebrews 11:24–27 NIV

Moses saw "him who is invisible." As single parents we need to keep our eyes on the One who is invisible.

Single moms and dads today can learn grace, humility, and gratefulness when dealing with stepmoms or stepdads helping to raise their children. Single fathers or stepdads can learn to appreciate the difficult role each mother is placed in when trying to share a child.

Dads, have you thought and prayed about how you will handle with dignity lifting up and honoring your child's birth mother if you decide to remarry or date? Whether you have a relationship with your child's mother or not, it's important to remember you still play an important role in your child's life. Focusing on the Lord, as Moses did, is key.

We know that Christ died on the cross to save us from our sins and from ourselves. After He rose, He left the Holy Spirit here to intercede for us, to guide us, and to draw us closer to the Lord. Open the Word this week and allow the Holy Spirit to fill your mind and thoughts toward Christ. Get to know the Lord and share that knowledge with your children.

Here are a few Scriptures to get you started:

- Joshua 1:9 (ESV)—"Have I not commanded you? Be strong and courageous. Do not be frightened, and do not be dismayed, for the Lord your God is with you wherever you go."
- Psalm 119:116 (NLT)—"Lord, sustain me as you promised, that I may live! Do not let my hope be crushed."
- Isaiah 40:31 (KJV)—"But they that wait upon the Lord shall renew their strength; they shall mount up with wings as eagles; they shall run, and not be weary; and they shall walk, and not faint."
- 1 Chronicles 29:11 (TLB)—"Everything in the heavens and earth is yours, O Lord, and this is your kingdom. We adore you as being in control of everything."
- Psalm 143:8—"Let the morning bring me word of your unfailing love, for I have put my trust in you. Show me the way I should go, for to you I lift up my soul."

GOING DEEPER

1. What happens when a mother has to share her child with another woman?

2. Can you think of ways a parent usurps God's design for a child?

3. What are some ways you can handle sharing your children with someone other than their birth parent, when the time comes?

4. Some situations can cause a single parent to want to get involved with what is happening in the other home, such as inappropriate lifestyles of friends, different religions, etc. How can you prepare yourself and your children for these challenges?

5. Make a list of positive things you can do to influence your children to follow the Lord.

6

Living Faith in Desperate Times

The Faith of the Canaanite Woman

I was sitting at my desk one morning at my child care job when the phone rang. It was one of our parents. She was distraught and almost in tears. Her son had major behavioral issues and needed a lot of extra care. He had come to our early childhood program at three years old, having been sent to our program by a local therapist when he only had eight words in his vocabulary. Through a lot of patience and the special techniques that my teachers and I used, this child had come a long way.

Now the little boy was in public school in a special-needs classroom. He was doing pretty well for the most part. Mom was trying to apply for SSI (Supplemental Security Income) disability benefits for her son. She was barely making minimum wage. It was costly raising a child with special needs, plus she had an older son, and she was the sole provider for both boys.

She was calling because her son had been denied SSI. She was in tears and didn't know how she was going to survive. This parent was a relatively new Christian. She had found Jesus and was turning her life around. Her son was learning to communicate, and Mom was trying as best she could to live a Christian, faith-based life. But this situation was confusing to her. She had prayed and asked God for help, and since her salvation, we had talked and prayed with her many times. One time as we talked, the Lord planted in my mind just what I needed to say. (Isn't that just like God?) "Trish, have you ever heard of Elijah in the Old Testament? Your stress reminds me of Elijah. In 1 Kings, Elijah was experiencing a stressful time. He too was asking God for help. When Elijah went to meet the Lord, several things happened.

"It says in 1 Kings 19:11–12, 'Then a great and powerful wind tore the mountains apart and shattered the rocks before the Lord, but the Lord was not in the wind. After the wind there was an earthquake, but the Lord was not in the earthquake. After the earthquake came a fire, but the Lord was not in the fire. And after the fire came a gentle whisper.'

"God wasn't in any of the big things that happened on the mountain that day—no, God spoke to Elijah in a gentle whisper and in the calm and quiet time. God might want to speak with you in this manner too. Maybe God wants you to pull into yourself and get away from work, from all the noise and even from the confusion you are feeling.

"Find a place to just sit and think about God. Thank Him for saving you. Thank Him for all He has done for you and your boys. There are times when God is a gentle God. You have been through a lot, so get away from the wind, the earthquakes, and the fire, so to speak, and wait for God's gentle whisper."

Trish called me later that day. She was elated. She had taken my advice. She had gotten with God. She was calm and peaceful when she went back to work. Later in the afternoon she had gotten a call and was told there had been a mistake and her son now qualified for SSI. At the time, this was unheard of. If you were denied SSI, it took forever to reapply, and there was a lot of paper work that had to be filled out and refiled.

The Canaanite Woman and Her Faith

When we have an ill child or when there is some type of trauma going on with our child, most of us will do just about anything to get the attention our child needs. We read about such a situation in Matthew 15:21–28. There was a Canaanite woman whose child was suffering from demon possession. Can you imagine what that must have been like?

One day Jesus was leaving a particular region when a woman came running up to him, asking for mercy for her daughter. Let's see how her faith in Jesus played out.

> Leaving that place, Jesus withdrew to the region of Tyre and Sidon. A Canaanite woman from that vicinity came to him, crying out, "Lord, Son of David, have mercy on me! My daughter is suffering terribly from demon-possession."
>
> Jesus did not answer a word. So his disciples came to him and urged him, "Send her away, for she keeps crying out after us."
>
> He answered, "I was sent only to the lost sheep of Israel."
>
> The woman came and knelt before him. "Lord, help me!" she said.
>
> He replied, "It is not right to take the children's bread and toss it to their dogs."
>
> "Yes, Lord," she said, "but even the dogs eat the crumbs that fall from their masters' table."
>
> Then Jesus answered, "Woman, you have great faith! Your request is granted." And her daughter was healed from that very hour.
>
> Matthew 15:21–28

This story is interesting in that Jesus was trying to keep His presence in the village quiet. He had been performing miracles and healing people. He wanted to avoid the opposition and continue to teach His disciples. He had much teaching to do before He faced the cross. But the Canaanite woman had already heard about Jesus, and she needed Him to help her.

The version of this same story in Mark says, "In fact, as soon as she heard about him, a woman whose little daughter was possessed by an evil spirit came and fell at his feet" (Mark 7:25). This woman was desperate for her daughter to be healed of the evil spirit.

We have all faced discouraging or desperate times. It might be not having enough food. It could be the loss of child support, the loss of a job, or just an event at your child's school that you can't get off work to attend. Most of us just roll with the punches and keep on going. We just do the best we can at the time. This Canaanite woman knew she needed Jesus, but it is important to realize this woman also knew that she was a Gentile and that Jesus had come to preach and heal the Jewish people. But she was undeterred. Not even the disciples could keep her from approaching Jesus, the Jewish healer.

"The woman was a Greek, born in Syrian Phoenicia. She begged Jesus to drive the demon out of her daughter" (Mark 7:26). Because this woman addressed Jesus as "Lord, Son of David" (Matthew 15:22), she knew who some were saying Jesus was—"Lord, Son of David" was the popular Jewish title for the coming Messiah.

This woman must have loved her daughter very much to have come to the Jewish Messiah to beg Him to heal her daughter.

What can we glean from reading about this woman?

- She was a mom who was willing to fight.
- She was willing to argue.
- She was willing to beg for her daughter's healing.

This woman was ferocious when it came to the welfare of her daughter. Most of us in today's world don't have to go against society to get help for our children. Oh, you might have to go against the opinions of your family, friends, co-workers, or even your church family, but for the most part we don't have to face down our society at large.

The Canaanite mom had the faith needed to approach Jesus, and she believed in Him. She even had the audacity to continue to pursue Jesus when He didn't respond to her.

Do you think it was wrong for the Canaanite mom to be brave in pursuing Jesus? Keep in mind that in the society she lived in, women were not to speak out and approach men in public. It would have been especially inappropriate for a Gentile woman to address a Jewish man.

How many times have you had the audacity to pursue Jesus even when He didn't respond to you?

In Matthew 15:23 the disciples urged Jesus to send this woman away because she kept crying out after them. However, Jesus used this opportunity to allow her to demonstrate her faith in Him. "'First let the children eat all they want,' he told her, 'for it is not right to take the children's bread and toss it to their dogs'" (Mark 7:27).

Jesus was saying that the Gospel must first be given to the Jews. This Canaanite mom understood what Jesus was implying, probably because she understood He was the Messiah to the Jews, but she was willing to settle for anything Jesus would give her—even the crumbs.

She argued, "Yes, Lord, . . . but even the dogs eat the crumbs that fall from their masters' table" (Matthew 15:27).

"Then Jesus answered, 'Woman, you have great faith! Your request is granted.' And her daughter was healed from that very hour" (Matthew 15:28).

Stressful Lives[1]

The Canaanite woman must have been under tremendous stress. Evil spirits possessed her daughter, and she had no way of healing her. But this story could have had a different outcome. When some people are under stress, the stressful situation becomes their main focus, and instead of having faith in our Savior and our God, they allow the stress to take over.

Stress is the body's way of reacting to challenging events. Stressors can come in many forms for the single parent. But divorce or the sudden loss of a parent to death can also cause stress in children. Stress in adults and children can affect them

- physically,
- emotionally,
- mentally, and
- spiritually.

For children who are dealing with divorce, separation, or loss of a parent to death, stressors can include the following:

- Not knowing where the other parent is
- Wondering if the deceased parent is in heaven
- Trying to figure out who is picking them up after school
- Wondering where they will spend holidays
- Worrying about how to handle birthdays
- Not knowing what to do about the parents' new relationships
- Losing friends, pets, and holidays with extended family

All these things can leave children overwhelmed and unable to cope with life.

Children of divorce will experience many stressful moments—and for some, many stressful years—after their parents' divorce or separation. Every time a child has to change homes can be stressful. Each time a child hears one parent talking to the other in a certain tone of voice can produce stress. Hearing the words *lawyer*, *court*, *custody*, and *child support* can cause stress for the child.

For some people, the first reaction to a stressful event is a feeling of being threatened or a sense of fear. Any of the following events could produce this kind of stress:

- In the middle of the night your daughter's temperature suddenly shoots up to 104 degrees. What do you do?

- You answer the phone, and the sheriff tells you your child has been involved in a car wreck.
- Before you walk into the grocery store to buy a week's worth of groceries, you check your balance online, and there are no funds available. Then you wonder how you are going to pay for all the needed grocery items.
- Your son comes home and informs you he is going to live with his father. You fall apart trying to figure out what to do.

Illnesses and diseases can also trip us up. Even hearing the word *cancer* when getting the doctor's report about your parent can be stressful.

Whatever the situation, your response might be one of fear or perceiving a threat to you or your child's well-being.

The body's immediate response to a perceived threat is to channel resources for strength and speed. The brain dulls the body's sense of pain and looks for a path to safety.

- The heart rate speeds up, the pulse begins to race, and the racing pulse sends extra blood to the muscles and organs.
- Blood vessels open wider to allow more blood flow to large muscle groups.
- Blood goes to the large muscles in the legs, making the hands colder and preparing the body to flee.
- The pupils dilate for better vision, and lungs take in more oxygen.
- The bloodstream brings extra oxygen and glucose-fuel for power. Blood pressure rises.
- Adrenal glands secrete the fight-or-flight hormone epinephrine (adrenaline), and digestion halts, allowing the body to dedicate energy to the muscles. (Stomachaches are a common complaint in children who are under a lot of stress.)
- Finally, sweat is produced to keep the body cool.

I remember a stressful experience with my own son. I had taken him to a small clinic one Saturday morning. They took one look at him and had me rush him to the emergency room at a local hospital. When the surgeon examined him, he said, "This swelling could be several things. The first thing it could be is a cancerous tumor . . ." I'm not really sure what was said after that because I felt a rush of blood throughout my body. I think I experienced all of the symptoms mentioned above.

Because I was a single mom and totally responsible for my son, I had to quickly get ahold of myself and my emotions and calm myself down. I have a strong faith, so I went to the Lord and immediately asked God to take over and provide comfort and guidance. I couldn't lose it. I couldn't let the stress take over.

Another experience happened with my daughter. The summer after she graduated from high school she went on tour with a drum corps. Late one afternoon I got a call from a stranger somewhere in Alabama. The person on the other end of the line said, "I'm a chaperone on the drum corps, and your daughter, Julie, just passed out on the field. We had to call an ambulance and rush her to a hospital." Again, my body reacted to the stress.

I had to rein in my panic. I had to confidently think through several issues:

- Was she okay?
- How were they treating her?
- Why didn't the doctor at the hospital call?
- How would I get to her?
- What was wrong with her?
- Why did she pass out, and what did they mean by "pass out"?
- Was she unconscious?

The questions were endless and the answers few. Thanks to a special friend who purchased an airplane ticket, we were able to get her back to Oklahoma. She wasn't as bad as they originally thought. The chaperone thought she would be okay flying home without me. The Lord opened the door to get her immediately into a heart specialist in Tulsa, Oklahoma.

I know many of you are facing worse situations. When we are under stress, though, even the smallest thing can send us over the edge. When that happens, our bodies react quickly and efficiently to the perceived or real threat.

What Living under Constant Stress Does to Us[2]

Some milder forms of stress can keep us alert and allow us to do well in various situations. The brain and the body quickly return to normal once we are through the event. However, it is when we live in a constant state of alertness or chronic stress for long periods of time that we can be adversely affected.

Signs of poorly managed stress, chronic stress, or stress overload include the following:

- inability to concentrate
- poor memory
- low level of creativity
- flushed face
- cold hands
- rapid, shallow breathing
- disorganization—you can't find anything
- poor time management—you can't estimate time
- every task becomes overwhelming
- inability to have empathy—everything is about you
- no impulse control—you react
- poor motor coordination
- shortness of breath
- dry mouth

- acid stomach
- gas and diarrhea
- frequent urination
- palpitations
- irritability
- overindulging

When I speak at single-parent events, I often say that it's not unusual for single parents to be late all of the time. Because we are under stress, we can't estimate time. Almost always a few single parents will come up and share how they are always late. I tell them to slow down and think through the situation.

As single parents, all of us have experienced some of the symptoms above. It is when we live with these symptoms on a daily basis that long-term damage can occur. Under constant stress, we catch more colds and suffer other ailments. We also can't think as well at work or organize tasks efficiently. Emotionally, we're all over the place—we often get our feelings hurt or think people are judging us.

Finally, our faith may wane, or when we pray we don't feel like God is hearing us. Living with the results of constant stress can influence one's spiritual walk. It reduces the ability to concentrate on Scriptures and Bible studies. It interferes with our ability to pray. It can usurp our relationship with God if we allow it to.

When you are under chronic stress, one of the most important things you can do to reconnect with God is to set aside some quiet time for yourself.

When my kids were teens, I'd get up really early to pray and read my Bible. We lived in Oklahoma where winters can get pretty cold. We had a two-story house, so I'd set the thermostat low downstairs at night to conserve energy. Early every morning, I'd turn up the thermostat and get a cup of hot tea, my Bible, and my journal, and then I'd sit down on the heat vent. I'd wrap up in a big blanket, and the heat would blow up around me. Many mornings I'd end up falling asleep.

For years it bothered me that my kids would come downstairs and find me asleep. It also concerned me that I was sleeping through my time with God. Goodness knows I needed His assistance! One day I was talking to a friend, and she said, "Don't be so rough on yourself. Your kids knew you were trying, and the heavenly Father knew you were giving it all you had. And what better place to rest than in the arms of God?"

Some other ways you can connect with God:

- Play praise and worship music during the day.
- Listen to a recorded version of the Bible as you are driving.
- Connect with other single parents and share a verse that impacted you this past week.
- Write out Scriptures on Post-it Notes and place them all over your home.
- Attend church.

In the blog post "How Going to Church Benefits Brain and Body,"[3] Charles Stone, a pastor in Canada, writes that "God wired our bodies and brains to benefit from both attending church and developing a healthy spiritual life." If the church "is filled with kind and caring people," he writes, then the brain releases the hormone oxytocin. This chemical helps you bond with other people. Also, attending church can lessen one's depression, and people who attend church handle pain better and are less likely to commit suicide.[4]

But back to our discussion of the Canaanite mother. We can all learn from her faith, which gave her

- courage to speak up,
- incentive to seek out Jesus, even when the disciples were discouraging,
- understanding of what Jesus was implying, and
- a healed child.

"Then Jesus answered, 'Woman, you have great faith! Your request is granted'" (Matthew 15:28).

How is your faith? Sometimes as single parents we need someone to walk alongside us and be honest with us when we are facing stressful situations. We need someone we can call to pray with us during these stressful times.

We need the faith of the Canaanite mother. "Now faith is being sure of what we hope for and certain of what we do not see" (Hebrews 11:1).

GOING DEEPER

1. Journal about a time when you had to step in and face adversity, or go against society, or even go against the opinions of friends or family regarding the welfare of your child.

2. Journal about a time when you continued to pursue God regarding a concern about your child when you thought He wasn't listening to you or it seemed He wasn't answering your prayers.

3. Was it wrong for the woman to settle for the crumbs that fell to the dogs under the table? Why or why not?

4. Write about a time when Jesus allowed you to demonstrate your faith in Him regarding the care of your children or something else to do with one of them.

5. Think of a time when you felt your body react to a stressful event. Which of the responses listed in this chapter did you feel happening in your body?

6. What does your faith under ongoing stress look like?

7

Reaching Out
and Being Vulnerable

Asking for Help

She came to a picnic, but she stood off to the side. She watched
her kids but didn't attempt to interact with the other single parents. At the end of the evening, she packed up her kids, barely
said good-bye, and left. There was something different about
her. I couldn't put my finger on it, but something was definitely
bothering her.

All night I kept thinking about this lady. The Lord would not
let go of me, and the next morning I called a pastor friend and
said, "I need for you to go visit a single mom[1] with me today. We
need to go as soon as we can. I'm really worried, and the Lord is
telling me we need to go see her."

He consented to meet me at the lady's apartment.

She invited us in, and her apartment was immaculate. Now, she
had three children, so by all rights, her apartment shouldn't have

been that clean. Two of the kids were at the apartment park, and her toddler was taking a nap.

I asked how she was doing, and she said, "Oh, I've just been cleaning and putting things in order." When she said that I knew what was going on. She was planning on taking her own life. That is why the Lord wouldn't let go of me. He knew.

As my pastor friend talked to her, I checked out her fridge. It was empty. No food for her kids. No milk, nothing. I looked in the kitchen pantry, and it was basically empty. I checked on the toddler, who was sound asleep. There were no toys, no clothes anywhere. It was eerie.

As she talked, her story began to reveal the full truth of her situation. Her husband had come home from a trip and told her he was moving out and relocating to another city with his partner. He revealed he was gay and had been for a long time. He packed up his belongings and left the family. He left her no money, didn't want the kids, and abandoned her and their family. She explained she didn't know how she was going to feed her kids. Eventually she told us she had planned on taking her life after she put the kids to bed that night.

Right away, my friend had some food brought in. We contacted relatives to come and stay with the kids, and we had the mom hospitalized. This was a mom who couldn't ask for help. Evidently, because of the shock of finding out her husband was gay, her brain shut down and she couldn't think her way out. She was vulnerable and in shock.

Single parents, for the most part, are an independent group. We have to be in order to survive and parent our children alone. Sometimes it is okay to ask for help. Sometimes it is necessary to ask for help.

Sometimes we are too proud to get help, and our children suffer. I was one of those "too proud" people. More than once the Lord had to teach me it wasn't about me but about my kids, and sometimes it was about being an example to other single parents.

Elisha and the Widow

In my opinion it takes a lot of energy and bravery to ask for help. I've worked with and ministered to single parents for more than fifty years, and just about the time I think I've experienced every situation, something new pops up. But while I think it is a new situation, really, every situation is covered in some form in God's Word. The story of the woman who approached Elisha about the creditors coming to take her kids to pay her dead husband's bills is a unique single-parent story and is one from which we all can learn.

In 2 Kings 4:1–7 we read,

> The wife of a man from the company of the prophets cried out to Elisha, "Your servant my husband is dead, and you know that he revered the Lord. But now his creditor is coming to take my two boys as his slaves."
>
> Elisha replied to her, "How can I help you? Tell me, what do you have in your house?"
>
> "Your servant has nothing there at all," she said, "except a little oil."
>
> Elisha said, "Go around and ask all your neighbors for empty jars. Don't ask for just a few. Then go inside and shut the door behind you and your sons. Pour oil into all the jars, and as each is filled, put it to one side."
>
> She left him and afterward shut the door behind her and her sons. They brought the jars to her and she kept pouring.
>
> When all the jars were full, she said to her son, "Bring me another one."
>
> But he replied, "There is not a jar left." Then the oil stopped flowing.
>
> She went and told the man of God, and he said, "Go, sell the oil and pay your debts. You and your sons can live on what is left."

Let's take a moment to take this story apart. What does "company of the prophets" mean? The NIV Study Bible reference note for 2 Kings 4:1 leads us to 1 Kings 20:35, and in the note for that verse we learn that a group of prophets were religious men who grouped together,[2] and in this instance they were dedicated to Elisha and considered him their mentor. The wife referred to her husband, who was part of the company of prophets, as Elisha's servant or follower. Her husband loved, respected, and was dedicated to the Lord.

We can learn from this widow that it is important to know whom to approach for help. It is also important to note that she wasn't hesitant or shy about stating her case.

First of all, she approached the prophet. Second, she reminded him that her husband was one who served the prophet. Third, she stated her need: There was a debt, and the creditors were coming to take away her boys to be slaves until the debt was paid.

Mosaic law allowed for servitude as a way to pay debts (Exodus 21:1–2). So when she said, "to take my two boys as his slaves," it literally meant that they were going to take her sons and make them slaves to pay off the debt. Can you imagine someone coming to your home and saying, "Hey boys, pack up your belongings; tell your mom good-bye. You are going to be our slaves and work for us"?

At this time in history, women had no way of earning money. The creditors must have been ruthless. Imagine what this mom must have been going through—grieving, worried, and maybe even panicked. Personally, I don't think she felt sorry for herself. She knew she had to do something. If she had been too proud to ask for help, her boys would have suffered.

It is important to notice that the prophet of God didn't just give money to this woman to pay her debts; he wanted her to be a part of the solution. Elisha asked the woman what she wanted him to do. Then he asked her what she had in her house.

The prophet told her to ask her neighbors for a lot of empty jars, go inside, shut the door behind her and her sons, and pour the oil into the jars. As each was filled, she was to put it aside until eventually all the jars were full. It is amazing that when all the jars were gone, the oil stopped flowing. Isn't that so like God?

After the Oil Ran Out

After the oil ran out, the widow went back to Elisha for more instructions. She probably said something like, "We used all the jars. The oil stopped flowing; now what do I do?"

The man of God then told her to sell the oil and go pay all of her debts and live on what was left over.

Oil was a very precious commodity back then. It was probably olive oil that the widow had reserved for cooking. She ended up with enough oil to keep her sons from being sold into slavery and enough left over to live on after all the debts were paid.

Types of Needs

Many single parents need financial assistance, but there are other areas of need as well. Perhaps you are a dad who needs help finding your daughter a certain dress or costume for a play.

Or you are a dad and your daughter has her first menstrual period. What do you know about shopping for this stuff? Do dads even do this? William, a father of three children, says, "Yes, I was the dad who went in the store and bought stuff for my daughter's menstrual period." A brave man, for sure.

Or maybe you wake up to find the water supply line to your water heater has ruptured, and you are clueless about what to do while the water is spewing all over the house.

Or maybe you are a single mom, and your son asks about dating.

How do you handle these kinds of situations by yourself? Like the widow in our story, you trust God and you ask for help.

What Can We Learn from the Widow?

Everyone has problems or situations that require outside assistance, and we can learn from this widow how to go about getting our needs met.

First of all, the widow approached the prophet. Know where to go for assistance and whom to ask. Do you go to the senior pastor of your church? Or do you go to the head of a certain ministry or committee?

Do you go to a government program such as welfare? Some single parents will need temporary help from the government, and there is nothing wrong with this. But first pray about where and to whom the Lord would have you go.

I know a lot of single moms and dads who are receiving government assistance through various programs. Every state is different, so check to see what is available in your state. Be very cautious, though, because it is easy to rely too much on outside assistance.

I had a hard time asking for any kind of assistance. When I was a single mom, one day I got a call from the middle school counselor, who was concerned that my son was hungry. She said he was so skinny and that he kept eating food off other kids' plates. She knew I was a single mom and suggested I apply for the free or reduced lunch program.

I told the counselor that I gave each of my kids enough money for lunch and school supplies. I also told her I kept peanut butter and bread along with fruit and other lunch items if Brian chose to make his lunch. But after Brian and I talked about it, I opted to apply for the free lunch program. It was a humbling experience for me.

After approaching the prophet, the widow reminded him that her husband was one who served the prophet, and then she explained her situation. Explain to the person you are asking for help what has happened. Discuss what your needs are, and if you are in a crisis situation explain how you got there.

But also go before the Lord and remind Him that you are doing all you know how to do. Ask God what He would have you do. If you are serving Him, remind Him of your service. God knows you are struggling to raise your children, but He wants you to depend on Him and He wants you to ask Him for what you need.

"God is not unjust; he will not forget your work and the love you have shown him as you have helped his people and continue to help them" (Hebrews 6:10).

How do you think this Scripture applies to your life or your situation? Take a few minutes to pray about it.

The widow stated her need to Elisha, letting him know that she was in debt and that the creditors were coming to take away her boys to be slaves. State your case with boldness.

"Let us then approach the throne of grace with confidence, so that we may receive mercy and find grace to help us in our time of need" (Hebrews 4:16).

When you need help,

- know what you need,
- know how much you need,
- know when you need it,
- do your homework and be specific, and of course,
- pray about the need.

Bobbi, a single mom, came to church one Sunday morning. She parked her car, and just when she opened the door to get out, the back windshield exploded. She had no idea why. Thankfully her kids weren't hurt, but she was pretty shaken up when she came into church. Some of the men from the church walked out to her car to inspect it and calm her down. Since there was a lot of road construction going on at the time, the only thing the men from the church could figure was a large truck must have kicked up a rock that struck her back windshield. When she opened the door, it released just enough pressure to explode the windshield.

Later in the week she approached the church about helping her pay for it. She'd found out her insurance covered the front window but not the back. She brought an estimate from a local garage, and she knew how much she could afford and how long it would take to get it fixed. It was an older car and pretty expensive, but she had done her homework and was prepared. The men's Bible study class came up with the money to fix her windshield, and they were impressed by the research she had done beforehand.

Single Parents Need Help at Home

When the widow told the prophet what was in her house, he had some advice—she should include her sons. She could have excused her sons and tried to do it all herself, but she listened to what the prophet told her.

Many single parents tend to think they have to do everything or "juggle *every* ball," as Sandra Aldrich says in her book *From One Single Mother to Another*.[3]

Early on in my single-parent life, I learned I was going to need some help around the house. When my kids were eight and twelve, I took them into the laundry room.

I said, "Today I'm going to teach you how to do your own laundry. This is the washer, and this is the dryer." To which they replied, "Real funny, Mom. We know that." I went on, "But what you don't know is how to use them. So, I'm going to explain every detail of doing your own laundry."

I proceeded to explain how to sort the clothes, how to put the soap in the washing machine, when and how to add bleach, how to put clothes in the dryer, how to clean the lint trap, etc. I then told them that from that point forward they were going to be responsible for doing their own laundry.

My son jumped on this task right away, although I did have to go over it with him again later when I discovered he was washing one pair of pants or one shirt at a time.

On the other hand, my daughter went almost two weeks without washing her clothes. She came home one day and said, "Mom, my friends are starting to complain and say my clothes smell. I guess I better do my laundry." Now this would have been the time for many parents to chime in with all kinds of complaints and say, "I told you so," but I just listened and watched as she stuffed all of her clothes in the washing machine. (I knew that her red shirt was going to cause her white clothes to turn pink.)

Then she waltzed off to her room. The whole evening went by, and she never put her clothes in the dryer. I went to bed that evening wondering what would happen.

The next morning, as usual, she slept late. She rushed downstairs and shrieked, "Mom, did you put my clothes in the dryer?" She then crammed all of her clothes in the dryer at once. At this point it was really hard for me to keep my mouth shut. It was a cold winter morning in Oklahoma when she walked to the bus stop, standing there in jeans that were damp around the waist and down the seams. She had on a summer blouse she'd found in a drawer in her room and a lightweight sweater.

It was a hard lesson to teach and a hard lesson to learn. But later, as a military mom, my daughter taught all three of her boys to do their own laundry early on. The youngest was only four years old when he was doing his own laundry. Life lessons carried on to the next generation from this single mom!

Some single parents do all of the chores because they feel guilty for their poor little kids. If you are one of these single parents, you are not doing your children any favors. You are actually hindering their development.

Children need to learn to be part of *society*, and their society when they are children is your *family*. Children need to feel they belong. Russell Moore, in the article, "Parenting and Work: Helping Our Children Gain a Sense of Belonging," explains, "Work is a part of helping our children see where they fit in our family, in order to gain a sense of belonging."[4]

Contributing to something greater than yourself helps you to feel better about yourself. There is value in real work. Don't make up some easy task for your child, but give your child chores that fit his developmental level.[5]

The widow in our story had to work, and her sons had to help. This is a life lesson we can learn from the Bible. Take this lesson seriously and set up your household so that everyone assists with the chores. This concept also applies to parents who co-parent their children. Each home needs to allow the children to contribute.

Sandra Aldrich[6] writes in *From One Single Mother to Another,* "Counselors and child experts remind us that children who have time on their hands aren't happy. We know that those who have no chores and no responsibilities tend to quarrel much more than those who have to be busy around the home." It might be that the kids who don't take on any responsibility are bored. The parent in the home is exhausted and simply doesn't have time for the kids, so the kids quarrel and fight with each other.

More than likely if the widow in 2 Kings had collected more jars, she would have had more oil. The Lord knew how much oil the widow needed. He knows what you need. It can be hard not to compare our families with other families and wonder why ours hasn't been blessed in a particular way. But continue to trust God. Remember His words, "And the Lord said, 'I will cause all my goodness to pass in front of you, and I will proclaim my name, the Lord, in your presence. I will have *mercy* on whom I will have *mercy*, and I will have compassion on whom I will have compassion" (Exodus 33:19, emphasis added).

God is always there. That doesn't mean that God gives us all of our wants, but He does provide for our needs.

The story of the widow gives you a picture of how God can demonstrate privately and intimately His mercies to your single-parent family.

"Then you will call upon me and come and pray to me, and I will listen to you. You will seek me and find me when you seek me with all your heart" (Jeremiah 29:12–13).

The End of the Story

After Joseph and I helped the lady at the beginning of this chapter get help, we never heard from her again. Her relatives lived in another town, and they took in the mom and the kids. I have no ending to this story except to say the Lord directed me. I listened, and a deeply hurting single mom and her kids were helped.

"As soon as I pray, you answer me; you encourage me by giving me strength" (Psalm 138:3 NLT).

GOING DEEPER

1. When the woman realized the creditors were going to take her sons, what do you imagine were some of her thoughts? List some of the feelings and thoughts this mom must have had.

2. When Elisha asked the woman what she wanted him to do for her,

   • What did she say she had in her house?
   • What did Elisha tell her to do?
   • What was the purpose of Elisha's instructions?

3. If you are using this book as a study with others, make a list of things single parents need help with in our world today. Or make a list of things you and your children need.

4. If you are in a church that struggles with knowing how to provide for single parents, brainstorm some ways a church can minister to single parents through practical means. Examples include:

- Car care—provide light maintenance, such as oil changes, tire checks, etc.
- Clothes closet—collect slightly used clothing to sell at a reduced rate
- Food pantry—collect canned goods and have available for families in transition
- Concert sitters—members make themselves aware of children's concerts and offer to accompany the single parent to the concert or sporting event

5. Even though Scripture doesn't tell us the widow in our story went on to help other widows, wise single parents who have been helped will want to offer their services to the church. What are some ways you can give back after you have been helped?

8

Glorifying God
in Single-Parent Life

Nothing Is Impossible with God

Rebecca is a friend of mine. We met at church, and after she found
out part of my ministry is to single parents and the divorced, she
came to visit with me. She and I met several times while she was
trying to keep her marriage together. Rebecca is a woman of God
who loves her heavenly Father, and she agonized over what to do.
She prayed and consulted with more than one person about her
situation, but when she realized that her children were suffering,
that was when it was time for her to let go and let God reign in
her life, even if it meant facing a divorce.

I think you'll see through Rebecca's story that God can indeed
be glorified in the single-parent life.

Here it is in her own words.

*Every little girl has dreams about her wedding day. The dress,
the groom, the cake, the kiss—it is all on her mind as she
plans years in advance. But not this . . . not the deep feeling*

131

of regret. Of all the things that I had dreamed about on the day of my wedding, this feeling of deep regret certainly wasn't one of them.

The name-calling and degradation should have been enough for me to decide to walk away before walking down the aisle, but I chose to marry my abuser. I chose to commit my life to someone who wasn't committed to me, or to my safety. As the years passed, the abuse escalated and it was no longer just a harsh word but a shove, a choke, and a punch to the side and chest.

I asked myself "why" a million times in the last twenty years but I've yet to come up with a valid reason why I chose to stay in an abusive relationship. Maybe I was convinced that my dedication and prayers would change this man from abuser to dedicated, loving husband and father. Maybe I was convinced that God would perform a miracle even if the one He was performing the miracle on wasn't a willing soul. Maybe, just maybe, my love is what would finally change him.

I was married seventeen years to a man who was unwilling and unable to love me the way I deserved to be loved. From day one, I felt such heartache over my decision. Our lives were hard but I was determined to make this marriage work. I wanted to honor God by my dedication and I wanted to show this man that my love was unconditional. Year after year, the abuse continued.

My love and my dedication didn't change him, nor did my prayers. Although I knew that true, authentic change came from an inward desire to change, I was convinced that God would still change this man for me and our three children. And when that didn't happen, God and I had a deep conversation concerning my expectations of Him. He is God! He can do all, but if He forced himself on my ex-husband, He would be no better than my abuser who pushed himself on me and manipulated me many times throughout the years.

God is a gentleman and desires a relationship with people who truly want that relationship. Manipulation is of Satan, and God ever so politely asked me to step down from playing His role.

After seventeen years of abuse, I listened to God and walked away. The heartbreak was so severe, and I wasn't sure that I would ever heal, but I did. Although it was a long process, God was so good to me and so faithful to lovingly heal the brokenness inside.

I remember praying and telling God, "If this is your will, use it for your glory. Please don't ever allow this story to die within me without it changing someone's life."

After my divorce was finalized, I began ministering to abused women while I was still healing. I began speaking at different women's events and having many one-on-one conversations with women who needed advice and encouragement.

Although God never wanted His daughter to live in an abusive marriage, He is using the situation to present a new way of living for other women. He is showing me and others that there is healing and love on the other side of abuse. Nothing is impossible with God.

Rebecca

Can God Use Your Situation?

While Rebecca's story mainly applies to women, we know that men can also be emotionally and physically abused. We know that women can be just as controlling and abusive in some marriages.

How can men and women whose ex-spouses were controlling, manipulative, and sometimes downright mean honor God? Is it possible that these stories and lives can bring glory to the heavenly Father? Nothing is impossible with God.

Many parents consult friends, co-workers, and family, asking them what they think should happen with the marriage. Others go to counseling, hoping a counselor or therapist will tell them what to do. Sometimes a person will go to their pastor, hoping he will tell them what to do or give them a magic solution for changing the other person. As Rebecca finally realized, no one can make another person change.

When my ex-husband left, one of my son's teachers told him, "If you'd just pray harder, your dad would come back home." My son agonized over this. Eventually he came to talk to me about it. He said he had been praying really hard and wanted to know why God didn't make his dad come home. Was he not praying enough?

I explained to Brian that the Lord doesn't make people do things. God did not create us to be puppets He controls, or marionettes for which He pulls the strings. He loves us so much that He gives us the gift of free will. I said, "Even though God didn't want the divorce to happen, He allowed your dad to make his own decision. It has nothing to do with how hard you pray. And by the way, what exactly is hard praying? Is it better than easy praying?" With that, Brian smiled. This could have been one of those situations where I lambasted his dad or got angry with his teacher, but instead God allowed it to be a teaching moment when a little kid could be relieved of any guilt he might have felt about his home being disrupted.

As single parents, we have many opportunities to show our children about God's mercy and grace. Sometimes, with our busy and hectic schedules, we might not see those moments flash by, but ask the Lord to reveal them as they arise.

Other times God uses our story or our situation to change someone else's life.

Jesus Brings a Widow's Son Back to Life

There are many instances in the Bible where Jesus allowed a single parent's situation to glorify Him, such as this story found in Luke 7. Jesus was traveling, preaching, and teaching when He came upon a funeral.

Soon afterward, Jesus went to a town called Nain, and his disciples and a large crowd went along with him. As he approached the town gate, a dead person was being carried out—the only son of his mother, and she was a widow. And a large crowd from the town was with her. When the Lord saw her, his heart went out to her and he said, "Don't cry."

(vv. 11–13)

Even a large crowd of friends could not console this mom in her grief. Her son was dead, and they were carrying him to be buried. The Lord's heart went out to the mother, and He had compassion on her. God loves the single parent.

Then he went up and touched the coffin, and those carrying it stood still. He said, "Young man, I say to you, get up!" The dead man sat up and began to talk, and Jesus gave him back to his mother.

(vv. 14–15)

Jesus gave the woman her son. He could have called the son to come follow Him, but He knew the woman needed him. God is sensitive to the single parent.

They were all filled with awe and praised God. "A great prophet has appeared among us," they said. "God has come to help his people." This news about Jesus spread throughout Judea and the surrounding country.

(vv. 16–17)

This situation brought glory to God. Can God use your situation to bring glory to Him? He probably does more than you realize. I'm finding out now, years later, how much my life impacted various single parents.

I remarried in 1997, and my husband died of cancer. This brought me into a new realm. I've always had the mind-set that if I have to go through something, then I want the Lord to use it to help others.

Several years later, a man from where I worked in North Carolina found out he had cancer, and I immediately connected with his wife. While every situation is different, I knew my story could help. After her husband, Vinnie, passed away, I got a note from her:

As stuff settles and I ease into some kind of normal life, accepting each day that I have a new role in life, I cannot help but think back on all the advice you gave me on this journey! I cannot even begin to tell you all the things that come to mind—the power of attorney papers, the will, the conversation with family, the signs and preparations. It was invaluable and as I've said before, I hope to pass [it] on to someone else one day.

Gail Sanseverino

Gail has passed on what she learned in her time of struggle, and now hundreds of widows and widowers are being helped as she brings hope and encouragement through her ministry, The Widow's Peek. Here is what she says on her Facebook[1] page about this ministry: "God's plan for The Widow's Peek has become increasingly clear over the first seven years of its birth: discipleship. Every resource we provide and continue to produce is meant to encourage the widow and widower to press on, to know that they aren't alone. God is working in their lives and hearts, and His people are cheering them on."

In the story in Luke 7:11–17 we don't know if the widow knew who Jesus was.

It appears this widow was well known in her city, as she had many friends with her. Being a widow meant she likely would have had to depend on her son to support her. You can imagine how overwrought she must have been.

The Jewish custom at that time was for the coffin to be open as it was carried. It is important to note that Jesus went up and touched the coffin, not the dead man. But He commanded the dead man to sit up, and he sat up and started talking. Think about this—if God's voice can do this, how much more should His Word be a source of comfort and confidence for us today? God's voice had power then, and His voice has power today. Jesus still speaks to us. While you might not hear an audible voice, He can speak in your heart, through your pastor, through godly friends and counselors, through music, and through His Word.

Elijah Brings a Widow's Son to Life

In the Old Testament there is another story about a child being raised from the dead. In 1 Kings 17:17–24, we read of Elijah bringing a widow's son to life.

> Some time later the son of the woman who owned the house became ill. He grew worse and worse, and finally stopped breathing. She said to Elijah, "What do you have against me, man of God? Did you come to remind me of my sin and kill my son?"
>
> "Give me your son," Elijah replied. He took him from her arms, carried him to the upper room where he was staying, and laid him on his bed. Then he cried out to the Lord, "O Lord my God, have you brought tragedy also upon this widow I am staying with, by causing her son to die?" Then he stretched himself out on the boy three times and cried to the Lord, "O Lord my God, let this boy's life return to him!"
>
> The Lord heard Elijah's cry, and the boy's life returned to him, and he lived. Elijah picked up the child and carried him down from the room into the house. He gave him to his mother and said, "Look, your son is alive!"
>
> Then the woman said to Elijah, "Now I know that you are a man of God and that the word of the Lord from your mouth is the truth."

Let's look at the parallels between these stories in the New Testament and the Old Testament:

1. Both women were single mothers.
2. Each was dealing with the death of a son.
3. People gathered around the bodies.
4. Each mother had a responsibility to take back her son after he was brought back to life.
5. Both Jesus and Elijah had concern and empathy for the mothers.

You can probably find other parallels that you can write about in the "Going Deeper" section at the end of this chapter.

Not about Faith

The story in the New Testament is not a story about faith. It is a story about Jesus' power and authority. It is a story about people being filled with awe at something Jesus did. It is a story that was talked about and told many times, and it spread throughout the area and even into the surrounding country. But through this story of Jesus' power, we develop our faith that He can be in control of our lives.

Have you ever wondered why you were experiencing trauma, crisis, or tragedy or even questioned why you were having a bad day? Sometimes what we are going through is not about us but about God. In John 11:1–44 the story about Lazarus being brought back to life isn't about Lazarus or Martha, but about Christ and that He was sent from God.

Jesus told Martha to open up the tomb where Lazarus had been dead for four days. Martha objected because she feared there would be a bad odor from the decaying body, but Jesus asked her in verse 40, "Did I not tell you that if you believed, you would see the glory of God?"

ARE YOU TEACHING YOUR CHILDREN to thank and praise the Father God when something happens in their lives? Do you model thanking and praising God?

Before Jesus brought the dead Lazarus back to life, He thanked His Father. Jesus knew to thank the Father, a lesson each of us can learn.

"Father, I thank you that you have heard me. I knew that you always hear me, but I said this for the benefit of the people standing here, that they may believe that you sent me" (John 11:41–42).

Think of a time when you were going through something difficult. Did you take time to thank Jesus that you might be influencing someone else through trials you were experiencing?

When you are in the midst of a trial, it might not feel like what you are experiencing is of any value, but look at the widow in the Luke account. Do you think she thought about how the loss of her son could be of any use to anyone? More than likely she was too upset to care about anyone else. Through the ministering of Jesus and the raising of her son, however, people were filled with praise for Jesus.

"They were all filled with awe and praised God" (Luke 7:16).

Rebecca, who started this chapter with her personal story, has gone on to influence hundreds of women who are being abused or have been abused. She has a closed Facebook page where she constantly encourages women to trust in God and to live their lives for the Lord. Who knew six years ago that her pain would be an encouragement to others? God knew.

Through our pain, our experiences, and living out our faith as single parents—both moms and dads—we can choose to glorify God. And when we do, not only do we help others, we also influence our children, and that will impact our children's children. Faith is the strongest heritage we can pass on to the next generation.

On Mother's Day, Emmi, Rebecca's thirteen-year-old daughter, sent her this message:

Dear Mom,

Thank you for being a role model to me. Thank you for making me stronger. Thank you for being an inspiration. Thank you for fighting for Tyler, Jacob and I. Thank you for protecting us. I am so so so blessed to have you for my mom and dad. When I get angry or upset, you always set an example by being calm and firm in our faith. When I become a mother, I aspire to be as loving and caring as you are. No matter how much we fight and argue (sorry for my attitude with you), you still love me. I appreciate all the things you have done to ensure our happiness. Thank you for literally being the BEST mom in the world. Happy Mother's Day.

Love, Emmi

GOING DEEPER

1. Why do you think Luke recorded these various facts in Luke 7:11–17?

   - There was a large crowd following Jesus.
   - As Jesus approached the city gate, He saw a dead person being carried out of the city.
   - This person was the only son of a widow.
   - A large crowd was with her.
   - Jesus felt compassion for this widow.
   - Jesus told her not to cry.

2. Have you ever known or found out later that something you were going through impacted another's relationship

with our heavenly Father? If so, journal about the situation and how you found out God was using you to impact His kingdom.

3. How has a single-parenting crisis, trial, or bad day you've experienced glorified God?

9

How to Cope with Irritations

A Single Parent's Plague of Locusts and Other Irritations

Melissa connected with me on a Wednesday evening at a prayer time in our church. This was one of those God-ordained situations. Because of another responsibility, I usually didn't attend the mid-week prayer time, but this particular Wednesday I was there when Melissa decided to visit. Something was said about single parents, and after the meeting she approached me.

Melissa was a single mom with two daughters. She had just gotten out of jail. She had found Jesus there—yes, this actually happens, and when it does, Satan doesn't like it. Like in the Old Testament story about Moses trying to convince Pharaoh to let the Lord's people go, Melissa had been plagued with many irritations. But in Melissa's situation, it was Satan causing the irritations. He just couldn't let Melissa go and live her life for the Lord.

When she got out of jail, she only had a few days to find a job, get a car, and secure a place to live, or she would lose custody of her two precious daughters. When I met her, she was working, had found a car, and was living with her daughters in a single rented room in a lady's home in our area.

I invited Melissa and her girls to join our single parents' monthly dinner the next week. When she walked into the restaurant, I could tell something was wrong. The lady who was renting her a room had just been killed in a car wreck that morning, and the woman's thirty-year-old son was living there and had brought in a lot of alcohol and was having a party that night. Melissa knew that if alcohol or any drugs were in the house when the state authorities came, she would lose custody of her kids.

The former foster mother of her daughters invited her to come and live in her home, so that problem was solved pretty quickly. But then her car went out. The church had a connection with one of the garages in our area, and we were able to convince the mechanic to give her a break on fixing her car. Meanwhile, her oldest daughter had problems in school and was diagnosed with ADHD (Attention Deficit Hyperactivity Disorder) and had to be put on medication.

Melissa was trying so hard to survive, but things just kept knocking her down. She struggled with knowing how to parent her daughters. Most of us parent the way we were parented, and Melissa had not had good parenting models.

Melissa is the desperate single mom from chapter 1 who had all of her things stolen from the storage unit. Right after our church was able to help her fill the storage unit back up, her car broke down again. We took up a collection and were able to help her get the car fixed again.

Satan just kept beating on her door. Melissa had been in foster care when she was young, and her parents eventually lost custody of her. She had been adopted when she was fourteen but always competed for her adoptive mom's attention with the mom's birth daughter. Her entire life had been filled with irritations, crises, and traumas. Now she was trying so hard to live a faith-filled life for the first time, and she didn't want her daughters to go through what she had.

Everyone experiences hardships and devastating situations, even though it might not seem that way. Sometimes we feel like we are the only ones. Or as single parents, we may know others are as stressed as we are, but we get so bogged down with our own problems that we have trouble caring.

Often this is because of all the locusts swarming around us—you know, the little things that become *huge* and overwhelming and devastating. Let's look in the book of Exodus and read about how God used Moses to bring devastation to Pharaoh.

The Israelites Were in Bondage—and Sometimes We Are Too

As single parents, we have to consider how we handle irritations. Do we let them harden us? Do we let them harden our children? What is God trying to teach us as He allows such irritations in our lives? Or how will He be glorified through them?

The people of Israel were in bondage to Pharaoh, the Egyptian king. (For a deeper understanding, read chapters 7–10 of Exodus.) God sent Moses to deliver His people. As we read the biblical text for this chapter, know that God had already brought a lot of disaster to the Egyptians, and Pharaoh had made concessions and promises, but each time Moses asked God to remove the plague, the Egyptian king went back on his word.

"Then the Lord said to Moses, 'Go to Pharaoh, for I have hardened his heart and the hearts of his officials so that I may perform these miraculous signs of mine among them that you may tell your children and grandchildren how I dealt harshly with the Egyptians and how I performed my signs among them, and that you may know that I am the Lord'" (Exodus 10:1–2).

God told Moses what he must do, "Go to Pharaoh," and He also told Moses that He had hardened Pharaoh's heart. Why would God harden Pharaoh's heart when He was planning to deliver His people?

Our last chapter addressed how we sometimes go through an experience not for ourselves but for someone else. Depending on how you handle a situation, your story may very well be told to your grandchildren and their children. That's a sobering thought!

There have been a few times in my single-parent journey that I didn't handle something very well, and now as adults my kids love telling those stories to my grandchildren.

Through Moses, God had already done several things to convince Pharaoh to let the people go. If you look back to Exodus chapters 7 through 10, you can see some of the ways God used Moses to convince Pharaoh to release the people of Israel—frogs, gnats, flies, hail, and the death of livestock.

But after all these plagues, God still hardened Pharaoh's heart. So Moses told Pharaoh that God would send locusts to his country and they would devour every tree the hail hadn't killed.

> If you refuse to let them go, I will bring locusts into your country tomorrow. They will cover the face of the ground so that it cannot be seen. They will devour what little you have left after the hail, including every tree that is growing in your fields. They will fill your houses and those of all your officials and all the Egyptians— something neither your fathers nor your forefathers have ever seen from the day they settled in this land till now.
>
> Exodus 10:4–6

At first, the locusts probably didn't seem all that bad. The Egyptians had experienced gnats, flies, frogs, hail, etc. How much worse could locusts be?

> So Moses stretched out his staff over Egypt, and the Lord made an east wind blow across the land all that day and all that night. By morning the wind had brought the locusts; they invaded all Egypt and settled down in every area of the country in great numbers. Never before had there been such a plague of locusts, nor will there ever be again. They covered all the ground until it was black. They

WHEN I SIGNED THE CONTRACT to write this book, I told my daughter to be aware that I was going to use stories from her life as a teen in examples. She said, "Remember, you have to change the name to protect the innocent." To which I replied, "Ah, but you weren't innocent." She came back at me with, "If you talk about me, then you have to promise to put the baseball bat story in your book!"

Ugh! So here is the bat story. It is not one of my finer moments.

Because we didn't have a lot of extra funds, when something broke down we often figured out how to get by without it. At one point, the dryer door latch broke. My son figured out that if we jammed a bat up against the door and anchored it on the floor, the door would stay closed and our clothes would dry.

One evening I came home dead tired. It had been a long, rough day at work. The kids had finished their homework and were in the living room watching TV, and I went straight to the laundry room, took the clothes from the washing machine, and put them in the dryer. I jammed the bat into the door, but just

devoured all that was left after the hail—everything growing in the fields and the fruit on the trees. Nothing green remained on tree or plant in all the land of Egypt.

Exodus 10:13–15

One can only imagine what that experience must have been like. All Pharaoh had to do was tell Moses to take the Lord's people and go, so Pharaoh called Moses and told him he had sinned against Moses' God. He asked Moses to forgive him and to pray to his God to take the deadly plague away and then Pharaoh would let the people go. Of course, we know that God again hardens Pharaoh's heart. God wasn't quite through with Pharaoh yet.

about the time I stepped into the kitchen, the bat fell down. I sighed and put the bat back against the door.

I stood there for a few seconds and all seemed well. I took a step toward the kitchen but didn't even make it out of the laundry room when the bat fell again. This time I sighed deeper and longer and jammed that bat into the door a little harder. I walked out of the laundry room and got halfway through the kitchen when the bat fell again. That was the last stressful event I could handle. I grabbed that bat and began beating that old dryer!

My kids came running into the laundry room. "Mom, Mom, are you okay?" I just kept beating that dryer. Julie threw her hands in front of her brother as if to protect him and said, "Better the dryer than us, Brian," as they both started backing up. By this time, they were both laughing at their mother beating a stupid dryer. When I saw them laughing, I broke down into a boisterous laugh myself. I don't remember this part, but Julie said that after I finished beating the dryer I came into the living room, sat down, and said, "Ah, I feel a lot better now!"

My Personal Plague

One of the "plagues" that affected me was dirty dishes piled up in the sink and on the counter. I'm not sure why this bothered me so much, but it did. My son was pretty good about keeping the dishes cleared when it was his week, but my daughter couldn't seem to care less when it was her week. It wasn't an earth-shattering thing, of course, and I was pretty good at holding my tongue.

I was great at not doing them myself until it came to the weekend when the kids would visit their dad. When I would get up on Saturday morning, I couldn't bear to look at the dishes, so I would end up doing them myself.

At that time, both my kids had jobs to bring in extra income. My daughter worked, kept her grades decent, marched in the band,

PARENTS, IT IS IMPORTANT to think through situations with your kids. You don't have to have hostile kids living in your home.

and stayed active in the church youth group. She had a lot on her plate. But so did I.

This small irritation could have become a *huge* thing if I had let it. I could have nagged her. I could have punished her. I could have made her brother do the dishes. None of these were viable solutions.

If I had nagged her, it could have driven a wedge between us. If I had punished her, it could have backfired and created a hostile teen. If I had taken that chore away and given it to her brother, it wouldn't have been fair to him, and she would no longer have been contributing to our family.

I sought the advice of a very wise youth counselor. He gave me some options that would allow her to retain her dignity and me to retain her respect for me as her mother. I prayed about the things he said and decided what I thought would be best.

I had a meeting with my daughter at a time when neither of us was rushed or tired and explained in a calm voice how upsetting it was to me to have to see dirty dishes all weekend. She said she really was trying, but she had so much homework every night. She intended to do the dishes but then she'd get sidetracked and put them off until the next night, and then before she knew it, Friday was here. She said she would try to do them on Fridays, but a lot of times her dad would come to get them and get upset if he had to wait. She promised to try harder.

PARENTS, IT IS SO VERY IMPORTANT to allow your child to keep their *dignity*. Teasing, harassing, or making fun of them does not help them feel good about themselves or about you.

I told her that I understood her dilemma, but still dirty dishes were a problem and often there were no clean dishes for me to eat out of all weekend. Then I told her, "I really do understand, so here's the deal. If you leave dirty dishes in the sink and go to your dad's for the weekend, then I will take your lunch money for the next week and use it to eat out all weekend. I will not do the dishes. And it will not be your brother's week to do dishes until you have cleaned up the kitchen. Is there any part of this you don't understand?" Always make sure your teen understands what has been said.

I'm sure you can figure out that the next time she went to her dad's I got to eat out all weekend. That was the only weekend I got to eat out. She didn't like having to make her lunch all the next week because she didn't have any lunch money. My daughter's heart wasn't hardened like Pharaoh's, but it could have been if I hadn't handled the situation with calmness, praying through it and thinking about how to handle it.

Your Personal Irritation

Take a few minutes to think about your personal irritations. (Record them in the "Going Deeper" section.) Perhaps your irritations have nothing to do with your children. One could be excessive traffic, which makes you overwrought, anxious, or angry by the time you get home. Some irritations are out of your control, but as an adult you are still responsible for how you respond.

When things are out of your control, it is important to seek the Lord. Ask for Him to guide you. Ask Him to show you how to respond. Throughout the entire story of the exodus of the Israelites, Moses always sought the Lord, knowing the power didn't come from him but from God. Don't you imagine there were times Moses wanted to throw his hands up and quit? Moses couldn't quit, and you can't either. You are the parent, and God has given your children to you. Your power must come from Him.

Pharaoh quickly summoned Moses and Aaron and said, "I have sinned against the Lord your God and against you. Now forgive my sin once more and pray to the Lord your God to take this deadly plague away from me."

Moses then left Pharaoh and prayed to the Lord. And the Lord changed the wind to a very strong west wind, which caught up the locusts and carried them into the Red Sea. Not a locust was left anywhere in Egypt.

Exodus 10:16–19

The west wind blowing the locusts away is an example of how even the "forces of nature are compelled to obey His sovereign will."[1] God is all-powerful and all-knowing.

In some situations, you might seek wise counsel, such as that of a pastor, youth minister, or youth counselor. Even with this counsel, it is up to you to think about, pray about, and evaluate what is best in your individual situation.

No matter what the irritation, God can be in control if you let Him. God can also get the glory. It may not seem like it at first, but hopefully someday you will see how God can be glorified in all things.

We will tell the next generation the praiseworthy deeds of the Lord, his power, and the wonders he has done. He decreed statutes for Jacob and established the law in Israel, which he commanded our ancestors to teach their children, so the next generation would know them, even the children yet to be born, and they in turn would tell their children. Then they would put their trust in God and would not forget his deeds but would keep his commands.

Psalm 78:4–7 NIV

I'm sure Melissa's two daughters will tell their children about the hard time their mom had and about how each of them found the Lord Jesus Christ as their Savior through those trials. Melissa eventually met a wonderful single dad in our church, and they are now married, and he is helping her raise her children. God is blessing her immensely. She is getting help understanding her past. She is journaling and coming to understand how things in her childhood have affected her own parenting abilities.

In jail Melissa had no hope until she met Jesus Christ, but through Christ there is hope. Melissa didn't give up. With all the irritations, she probably wanted to give up, but she knew she had a responsibility to her daughters and to the heavenly Father who brought her out of the murky waters of her childhood.

GOING DEEPER

1. Make a list of little things that become huge, take over your mind, interrupt your day, and affect your ability to parent effectively.

2. If you are reading this book with a group, choose one of these irritations and share what happens when you allow it to get out of control. What is the end result?

3. How does allowing that irritation to get out of control affect your ability to parent your children?

4. What options do you have to stop the irritation from taking over your mind, your heart, and your ability to be a caring parent?

5. If your end result in parenting through a situation was not good, what is another way you could have handled it that would have yielded a better outcome?

6. List things that are in your control.

7. List examples of things that are out of your control. It could be child support, the weather, traffic, things in the

neighborhood where you live, etc. After you make this list, write out beside each item what you can do to help yourself deal with these matters. Perhaps it just means taking a deep breath while you are in traffic or listening to praise music. It is your list, so record ways you can help yourself.

10

Learning to Depend on God's Timing

God's Timing Is Perfect

It can be hard to wait on God. I know you've felt that at some point in your single-parent life. My friend Sarah thought her life was perfect. She married her high school sweetheart and had a little boy, and then while he was just a toddler she got pregnant again. When she was giving birth to her daughter, her husband was out making another baby. Of course, Sarah was crushed. She now had a toddler and a newborn and was getting a divorce. She worked in the after-school program in the local elementary school, but that hardly paid enough to support her and her two kids.

Sarah was a Christian with a strong faith walk. At the time, she couldn't understand where God was during all of this. She had always depended upon God and followed biblical standards for her life, but this was just too much to comprehend.

Over the next few years, Sarah went back to school and got her degree. While she was in college, working in the after-school program, and caring for two very young children, she applied for a Habitat for Humanity house. She would have to put in 150 hours of labor to get her home. At Habitat for Humanity you don't necessarily work on your own house; you just have to put in the hours, and friends can help you collect the hours by working under your name. Her family and several of our single-parent friends at church helped her put in the hours to qualify.

As soon as she got her degree and had finished student teaching, she applied for a temporary teaching position. It was in the middle of the year, and she got the job, even though it is almost unheard of for a school to hire someone straight out of college and over other applicants with more experience. But the Lord knew Sarah needed this position. When the school year was over, they hired her full-time. All in God's timing.

Through all of this, Satan kept throwing up roadblocks. For instance, after Sarah had filled out the paper work for the house, she got a call from Habitat for Humanity at her after-school job telling her that if she was a single parent they would need a copy of her divorce decree. The problem was she didn't have the decree yet, and so she went home feeling rejected and alone. When she opened the mail, there was her decree.

Another setback was that when the Habitat award came through, the house was more than forty miles away. There was no way she could afford the gas or the time to travel almost an hour to school, day care, and work each day. Sarah had applied for a house in the area where she was working and in the school district where she had hoped to get a job; in a few weeks another house opened up in our area and Sarah got it.

When she moved into her house, some of us from church helped her paint the rooms, and others brought over furniture for her and the kids. In no time, her house was looking like a home. For Sarah, sometimes it was hard to wait on the Lord, and I know that many times she felt alone and desperate for companionship as she struggled over decisions. More than once I picked up the phone to hear her weeping on the other end.

God's Timing

The story about the widow of Zarephath in 1 Kings 17 can give single parents hope as we struggle. There are times when every single parent feels alone and desperate to survive and provide for his or her children. Through reading the story of the widow of Zarephath, you'll be able to see how God's timing is perfect for each situation. It is a story about how one single parent in the Bible listened to God and was able to develop ministering faith.

A little history before we read the story: Ahab was a very wicked king. In the first verse of chapter 17, Elijah explained to King Ahab, "As the Lord, the God of Israel, lives, whom I serve, there will be neither dew nor rain in the next few years except at my word."

The Lord then gave Elijah the following instructions in verses 2–8:

> Then the word of the Lord came to Elijah: "Leave here, turn east-ward and hide in the Kerith Ravine, east of the Jordan. You will drink from the brook, and I have ordered the ravens to feed you there."
>
> So he did what the Lord had told him. He went to the Kerith Ravine, east of the Jordan, and stayed there. The ravens brought him bread and meat in the morning and bread and meat in the evening, and he drank from the brook.
>
> Some time later the brook dried up because there had been no rain in the land. Then the word of the Lord came to him.

In verse 9 we first hear about the widow of Zarephath:

> "Go at once to Zarephath of Sidon and stay there. I have com-manded a widow in that place to supply you with food." So he went to Zarephath. When he came to the town gate, a widow was there gathering sticks. He called to her and asked, "Would you bring me a little water in a jar so I may have a drink?" As she was going to get it, he called, "And bring me, please, a piece of bread."
>
> vv. 9–11

Did you take note that out of all the people in Zarephath, he approached a widow, a single mother raising a child?

"'As surely as the Lord your God lives,' she replied, 'I don't have any bread—only a handful of flour in a jar and a little oil in a jug. I am gathering a few sticks to take home and make a meal for myself and my son, that we may eat it—and die'" (v. 12).

Why do you think this widow trusted in God? Do you think she had any hope that she and her son would be saved from death?

She must have been a caring mom, and she must have felt very alone. Her mind was on providing for her son and taking care of his needs, even though it might have been the last time she did. Still, she had the presence of mind to provide a jar of water for the man of God.

Here's what we can glean from this story:

- This woman must have had a lot of faith.
- She was living among pagan people in a pagan land.
- It doesn't appear that she was an Israelite, but she laid her life on the line in order to provide for the man of God, Elijah.

> Elijah said to her, "Don't be afraid. Go home and do as you have said. But first make a small cake of bread for me from what you have and bring it to me, and then make something for yourself and your son. For this is what the Lord, the God of Israel, says: 'The jar of flour will not be used up and the jug of oil will not run dry until the day the Lord gives rain on the land.'"
>
> She went away and did as Elijah had told her. So there was food every day for Elijah and for the woman and her family. For the jar of flour was not used up and the jug of oil did not run dry, in keeping with the word of the Lord spoken by Elijah.
>
> vv. 13–16

It's interesting to look at the order of the things the man of God tells this widow to do and what will happen.

1. Don't be afraid.
2. Go home.
3. Do what you said you were going to do.
4. But first make a small cake of bread for me.
5. Bring it to me.
6. Make something for yourself and your son.
7. The jar of oil and the flour are going to last until it rains.

God is a God of order. Even though we might not understand the order, He does things according to His plan. Sometimes it is hard to see that God has the situation in hand. We get impatient. We want things to happen on our time line. It can be hard to keep the faith and believe everything is going to work out in God's timing.

The man of God could have come after the woman had used up the flour and oil, but that wouldn't have been the order God designed for this situation—forcing her to be generous with her meager remaining food. God could have caused it to rain, but then the woman wouldn't have had to trust in the man of God. God always has a reason for His order. When we follow God's model of order, whether it is orderliness in our homes, in our thoughts, in our actions, etc., it can bring safety and calmness to our situation. Just as the man of God told the widow, don't be afraid.

Order Carried Over into Our Homes

A surprising aspect of patiently waiting on God's timing is living our lives with order. Order can be an important part of peace in our lives and can encompass many aspects of our home, including but not limited to clutter and messes, schedules, organization, and fights among siblings.

Consistent schedules can be difficult in single-parent homes, especially when kids are traveling back and forth between parents every other week. Organization can be hard for a single parent working long hours or overtime just to make ends meet. For some single parents, the stress, inconsistent schedules, children traveling back and forth, and disorganization can lead to clutter. I mean, who has time to clean?

There are studies that indicate disorder and clutter can cause anxiety.[1] But "rarely is clutter recognized as a source of stress in our lives," writes Sherrie Bourg Carter in the article "Why Mess Causes Stress: 8 Reasons, 8 Remedies": "Clutter bombards our minds with excessive stimuli (visual, olfactory, tactile), causing our senses to work overtime on stimuli that aren't necessary or important."[2]

A study by the Princeton Neuroscience Institute found that "when your environment is cluttered, the chaos restricts your ability to focus. The clutter also limits your brain's ability to process information. Clutter makes you distracted and unable to process information as well as you do in an uncluttered, organized, and serene environment."[3]

I know that when I first became a single parent, things in my house were a mess. I didn't have the energy to care what things looked like. But as time went on and I got healthy and strong, it dawned on me what a disaster my home was. Piles of clothes, piles of dishes on the kitchen counter, piles of papers and magazines and notes. All those piles made me anxious, and they also affected my kids.

I got busy and got things organized. My son was always an organized kid, keeping his little cars in a straight line, his stuffed animals just so in his bed, etc. But my daughter, now that was a different story. I always thought she was disorganized, but after she joined the air force I found out she just had a different system of organization than I did. In the air force, she received a special award for her organizational skills. I called her and said, "You got an award for your organizational skills? But your room was always a mess with clothes everywhere!" She replied, "I was organized. I had a pile of clean clothes, a pile of dirty clothes, and a pile of dirty-but-I-could-still-wear-them-if-needed clothes. My organizational skills are just different from yours."

Little children like and need order in their lives. When a parent dies, the order is gone. When a divorce happens, order is gone. Where there were two parents, now there is only one in the home. Some kids act out when there is no order, while others become anxious and nervous.

In our early childhood program, we had a three-year-old boy who suddenly began to display symptoms of OCD (obsessive-compulsive disorder). He had been a pretty happy-go-lucky little kid up until then. Previously, at nap time he would jump onto his mat, giggle, and go to sleep. But something changed, and at nap time, he would repeatedly smooth out his sheet and blanket, and he couldn't begin to nap unless everything was perfect. He started worrying excessively about things on his plate at lunchtime. His cup had to go in a certain place, and his fork had to be placed just so. We talked to his mom and dad, asking if anything was out of the ordinary. No, they said, everything was fine at home.

One weekend the boy's mom asked one of my teachers to baby-sit. When Miss Sue arrived at the home, she found all the dishes, pots, pans, and silverware dirty and stacked high in the kitchen. Takeout containers were strewn across the floor. The trash can was overflowing. We found out that Mom was mad because Dad wouldn't help at home. Dad was upset with Mom's nagging, so he quit doing anything around the home. Mom quit cooking and cleaning. Fighting between the parents was often and loud.

This child was caught in the adults' quagmire of selfishness. He began to try to order his world the only way he knew how—by keeping his things straightened up. The counselor we hired for our program explained that this little guy became obsessive about it to the point that he did develop OCD, all of it driven by disorder, stress, and his parents arguing all the time. By the way, the parents later divorced.

Disorganization on the Outside Causes Disorganization on the Inside

Some kids have frenzied or out-of-control behaviors. They may run around, jump over things, and leave their possessions strewn everywhere. Many of the children who act like this may have brains that stay in a constant state of confusion. Kids who act like this need an organized environment. You might say disorganization on the outside brings disorganization in their brains.

We proved this in our early childhood program and our after-school program. We kept an orderly environment with everything labeled and organized. There were no messes piled up in the corners. Games, arts and crafts, and science projects were neatly displayed on shelves.

At one point, more than 85 percent of our enrollment had been diagnosed with behavioral disorders; had been neglected, abused, or sexually molested; or were in foster care. Our kids needed to feel peace and comfort in our facility. "For God is not a God of disorder but of peace" (1 Corinthians 14:33).

Because of our success at accommodating out-of-control children and children with diagnosed behavior disorders, our program became part of a research program at Portland State University called Models of Inclusion in Child Care.[4] We were one of only ten programs in the United States to which they sent a research team. Amazingly, the research team could not pick out the kids with ADHD, RAD (Reactive Attachment Disorder), or ODD (Oppositional Defiant Disorder), etc.

The reason the researchers couldn't pick out these various children was the order we maintained in our facility. It was imperative for us to have an organized, clutter-free environment to bring calmness, a feeling of safety, and a reduction in anxiety. Our kids were calm. They knew where things were and where to put things back. This brought a feeling of pride and accomplishment because they were successful in helping maintain order. They felt safe because the staff members were calm and had things under control. Everything, on most days, ran like clockwork.

When homes are organized, kids can feel more at peace. Being at peace means less sibling fighting. Of course, being organized doesn't mean that all sibling arguing and fighting goes away—kids are kids—but it can limit the anxiety some feel, and that leads to calmer kids.

As a parent, it is important to take charge of your home and put it in order. Get your kids on a good schedule, recognizing that schedules change as kids get older.

We've already discussed kids contributing to the home, but I want to emphasize it again here. Kids need to keep their spaces organized and relatively clean.

They need an organized home so they can keep track of their homework and their belongings for school. They need an organized home so that when it's time to do one of those special school projects, Mom or Dad doesn't have to go out late at night to purchase tape and other supplies.

"When a country is rebellious, it has many rulers, but a ruler with discernment and knowledge maintains order" (Proverbs 28:2 NIV). **Your children are your people. Your home is your country, and it's up to you as the parent to maintain order.** It's also up to you to model faith in your home, which leads us back to the widow and Elijah.

Wavering Faith

If you are like me, you have had times where your faith wavered. You wanted to believe. You wanted things to work out. But because we are human, we get impatient. The widow in our story had a wavering faith, but again in God's timing, Elijah came through, and when he did he brought glory to God. We've read this part of the story in a previous chapter, but let's take another look.

> Some time later the son of the woman who owned the house became ill. He grew worse and worse, and finally stopped breathing. She said to Elijah, "What do you have against me, man of God? Did you come to remind me of my sin and kill my son?"
>
> "Give me your son," Elijah replied. He took him from her arms, carried him to the upper room where he was staying, and laid him on his bed. Then he cried out to the Lord, "O Lord my God, have you brought tragedy also upon this widow I am staying with, by causing her son to die?" Then he stretched himself out on the boy three times and cried to the Lord, "O Lord my God, let this boy's life return to him!"
>
> The Lord heard Elijah's cry, and the boy's life returned to him, and he lived. Elijah picked up the child and carried him down from the room into the house. He gave him to his mother and said, "Look, your son is alive!"
>
> Then the woman said to Elijah, "Now I know that you are a man of God and that the word of the Lord from your mouth is the truth."
>
> 1 Kings 17:17–24

The widow's faith, like that of many single parents, seems to have wavered in this crisis. When her son became ill and died, she thought it was because of her sin.

Some Bible scholars believe the woman might have thought Elijah's presence in her house had brought God's attention to her sin and that the death of her son was a divine punishment. She must have questioned why God, who had provided for and sustained the life of her son before, was now allowing him to die.

This is the first occurrence of someone being raised from the dead in Scripture. This widow, who was not one of God's chosen people, experienced a miracle. With this experience the widow knew for sure that Elijah was a man of God, and she now knew that the word of the Lord that Elijah preached was the truth.

Here is an important fact to note: This woman, who had not experienced all the miracles the Hebrew people experienced in the wilderness, had accepted Elijah and his God. God used this experience of her son being healed and her faith in the man of God to convince this widow that God is real and reliable.

In our world today, we don't have to go to prophets to ask for help. When Christ came to earth and was crucified, He left the Holy Spirit to intercede for us. We have the ability to pray to the Father through His Son, Jesus Christ. When we don't know what to pray, we can rest assured that the Holy Spirit knows and intercedes for us.

"In the same way, the Spirit helps us in our weakness. We do not know what we ought to pray for, but the Spirit himself intercedes for us with groans that words cannot express" (Romans 8:26).

So many times, single parents dwell on the *why* of a situation. The why questions can hold us back. Instead of asking why, ask *what*.

- Instead of "Why did this happen to me?" ask, "God, what do you want me to do about this situation?"
- Instead of "Why can't I move forward?" ask, "What am I going to do about moving forward? It is up to me to move forward in my life."
- Instead of "Why doesn't he love me anymore?" ask, "What steps am I going to take to heal from this heartache?"
- Instead of "Why is my son always getting in trouble at school?" ask, "What can I do to help my son do better in school?"

The *what* questions reframe our mind-set and put the responsibility on us, not someone else. It is a huge step for many people, but trust me—it will help you to move forward.

163

Keep in mind, God's timing is always perfect. Trust and believe in Him no matter what you are experiencing in your life and with your children.

In a crisis, it is important to remember that God has an order for how He is going to bring things about. If we try to take over and usurp God and His order, we can make the situation worse. Sometimes we have to wait on the Lord. No matter how much we might want God to come roaring through with mighty miracles, it rarely happens like that. God wants us to wait and trust Him. And many times, it's not for our benefit as parents but for our kids' benefit.

Sarah Does It Right

Our friend Sarah is doing so well. She celebrates every holiday with her kids. She and her kids decorate the house and the yard, and in the summer they plant a garden. Her kids help her cook and do chores. She and her best friend have taken the kids to Disney World more than once, and the two moms make T-shirts for each Disney day and plan way in advance what they are going to do there. She is an excellent fourth-grade teacher and gets all kinds of accolades from parents and the school staff. Was it hard for her to wait on God's timing? Yes, and there will be other hard times as her kids grow when she will have to wait on God's timing. But like the rest of us, she will do it because she loves the Lord that much.

GOING DEEPER

1. When was a time that you felt totally alone and desperate to survive?

2. Share with a friend about a time that you usurped God's order and made a mess of things.

3. What trial have you experienced where someone has come to encourage you to have faith that things would be okay?

4. How did they encourage you?

5. As you look back now, can you see a sense of order in the situation? List what happened in the order things came about.

11

Modeling Biblical Principles
for Children

Listen Closely to My Words

It was vacation Bible school week at Shelly's church. She was the children's minister, and like all children's ministers during VBS week she was busy—and things were hectic. Shelly was at work when she got the call, just after lunch on a Thursday afternoon, that her husband had been in a car accident and was being flown to the hospital. At around three o'clock she was told that he had died in the helicopter on the way to the hospital. They had started out the morning together; she had talked with him on the phone at around eleven, and now he was gone. So unexpected. How could this be happening?

After being told her husband had died, she walked down the hall, not knowing where she was, when the reality hit her.

She was a young mother left to raise their three children who were six, four, and two. Probably because she was a children's minister and a counselor, she understood more quickly than most that her kids were going to need help getting through this time.

She remembered the quote from Fred Rogers: "When I was a boy and I would see scary things in the news, my mother would say to me, 'Look for the helpers. You will always find people who are helping.'"[1] Shelly said the Lord impressed upon her to do something similar with her children.

Every time someone came to the house to help with something, she would say to her kids, "Do you know why Mr. So-and-So did that at our house?" They would say, "No," and she would say, "Mr. So-and-So loves God and loves us, and that's what you do when people are hurting. God sent him to help us." Over and over she told her kids this. She burned into their minds that the helpers were God's people. What a simple but ingenious way of putting biblical principles before her children. (I wish I had thought of this when I was raising my kids alone.)

Now they are teens, and every so often she hears them say, "That reminds me of when Daddy died and people came and helped us." Shelly was so afraid her kids would be angry that their dad had died so early in their lives. So far this doesn't seem to be the case.

Shelly kept her eyes fixed on Jesus, but her life was not without problems. Even strong Christian people and church staff members experience crisis and trauma. Shelly was blessed to have a church family that surrounded her, but still she was the one who had to raise those kids without a father.

When her daughter, Lexi, was in elementary school, other dads would come each year and take her to the father-daughter banquet. When Lexi was thirteen she went to the banquet and came home very upset because the speaker, who was probably trying to guilt the dads into giving their daughters more attention, had given statistics about what happens to kids who do not have a father in the home. Lexi was hurt and grieved about this. Similarly, when the fathers of Shelly's younger son's friends were coaching them in basketball, her son came home and said, "Mom, I wish my dad was alive to coach me."

Through Shelly's unyielding faith, her kids picked up and found their own faith walk. Without any prompting from her mom, her daughter put "Psalm 68:5" on her high school letter jacket. Lexi came to understand God was a "father to the fatherless." Maybe because she was a children's minister and had been to seminary, Shelly knew how to continually pump God's Word and principles into her children through simple stories on their developmental level. Having them attend a two-days-a-week preschool program at their church helped fill in the gaps.

She also kept some of the same traditions and rituals after her husband's death. When her husband put the kids to bed he would always end prayers with them by asking God to help them "grow big and strong and wise." Mom continued this ritual, giving them reminders that God loved them, which helped keep a relationship with their heavenly Father prominent in their young lives.

She taught her children to listen closely to what she was teaching them, and she kept them close to the Lord and to their church family. She allowed others to help her and her children. She allowed her kids to grieve and realized that as the kids aged, they would revisit the issue of missing their dad. She is a wise mom. The Bible gives us many examples of wise people.

A Wise Person's Words Help Us Understand Life

Solomon was wise, and it is thought that he wrote most of Proverbs. We can find our own wisdom by applying the author's words to our lives.

Let's read Proverbs 4:20–27 (NIV), and then we'll break the passage down and discuss how it applies to single parents' lives.

> My son, pay attention to what I say;
>   turn your ear to my words.
> Do not let them out of your sight,
>   keep them within your heart;
> for they are life to those who find them
>   and health to one's whole body.

I WAS CONSIDERATE OF MY CHILDREN when they were watching TV. I usually waited until a commercial, as I would expect them to do for me. You get back from your child what you model.

> Above all else, guard your heart,
>   for everything you do flows from it.
> Keep your mouth free of perversity;
>   keep corrupt talk far from your lips.
> Let your eyes look straight ahead;
>   fix your gaze directly before you.
> Give careful thought to the paths for your feet
>   and be steadfast in all your ways.
> Do not turn to the right or the left;
>   keep your foot from evil.

As a single mom, I came across this passage of Scripture during my morning quiet time, and for some reason it jumped out at me. I knew I needed to seriously consider this wisdom in raising my own children.

Have you ever said to your child, "Listen to what I am saying," or "Pay attention when I'm talking to you," or "Be quiet when I'm talking"? I remember trying to compete with the television when I first became a single parent, and then it dawned on me: When I wanted my kids' attention, I needed to walk over and turn off the TV or stand in front of it.

We want our kids to listen to us because we are usually

- trying to educate them or give them instructions,
- trying to build a stronger relationship with them,
- wanting to keep them safe,
- guiding them through tough times, or
- expecting them to carry out a chore.

As our heavenly Father, God is also trying to get our attention. In Proverbs 4:20 God is talking tenderly to us, and He is indirectly calling us His children when He says, in other words, "My son, listen to me because I have something important to tell you. I have these instructions for you and these commandments for you to live by." Let that sink in for a moment. He actually addresses us as "my son." That is a special privilege.

In verse 21, "Do not let them out of your sight, keep them within your heart," the author is referring to the words of God. God had given His chosen people His Word through prophets and by writing them on stones, as with the Ten Commandments. Up to this point, that Word had been external. But in several verses in Proverbs and in Jeremiah 31:33, God says He is going to put the commands in their minds and write them on their hearts.

"'This is the covenant I will make with the house of Israel after that time,' declares the Lord. 'I will put my law in their minds and write it on their hearts. I will be their God, and they will be my people'" (Jeremiah 31:33).

It is important to read God's Word, but His Word is also to be engraved on our hearts. When I wanted to get a point across to my kids or give them a Scripture, I would write it on their bathroom mirror. I'd use a dry erase marker so it would wipe off easily. At other times I'd put Scriptures on Post-it Notes in my car or around the house.

There is something about seeing Scripture every day that makes it begin to stick with you. I'd pick out a passage that related to a problem and made sense to my kids. Or the Lord would direct me to particular Scriptures to use with them or to help me parent my children in a particular situation. I wanted my kids to see God's Word brought to life and to experience how trusting in His Word brought wholeness and answers to life's problems.

Another way of applying Scriptures comes from Dr. Scott Turansky and Joanne Miller, RN, BSN. In a weekly Biblical Parenting Thought Exchange, they write,

Matthew 12:34 says, *out of the overflow of the heart the mouth speaks*. As you learn to listen to your child's heart, identify target areas that you sense are a problem. Behavior indicates what's happening inside, so when you see a particular weakness, jot it down on a piece of paper. You might list things like procrastination, pride, fear, gloom and doom, or lack of confidence.

You've probably known these character weaknesses were causing problems. By identifying the misconceptions at the root of the behavior, you'll be ready to do some deeper work in your child's heart.[2]

The Role of the Heart

In Proverbs 4:22 we read, "For they are life to those who find them and health to one's whole body" (NIV). Putting God's Word in our hearts gives us a new life and can affect our entire beings. Of course, we know what powerful emotions can flow from the heart as well as the brain. And those of us who are single parents raising our kids alone have also felt our hearts break. Sometimes our heads realize something, but it takes a while for our hearts to catch up. When Shelly was told her husband had died, her head heard it, and she acknowledged it, but the reality didn't set in until her heart felt it.

Anyone who has lost someone or experienced a broken relationship knows what it feels like to experience a broken heart. The heart is the center of our emotional being.

We are to guard our hearts and teach our children to guard theirs. Verse 23 warns us about this: "Above all else, guard your heart, for everything you do flows from it" (NIV). Most single parents have a deep understanding of the importance of teaching their children to guard their hearts, as many of us have watched as our kids' hearts were broken when one of the most important people in their life, their parent, walked out. Or when their parent passed away and the child didn't understand why that parent had to die. We want to protect our kids, but in some single-parent

171

homes, that's just not possible. We can, however, be there to help soothe the pain, and we do this by taking our kids to the Word of God.

Proverbs 3:1—"My son, do not forget my teaching, but keep my commands in your heart."

Proverbs 3:3—"Let love and faithfulness never leave you; bind them around your neck, write them on the tablet of your heart."

Proverbs 4:23—"Above all else, guard your heart, for it is the wellspring of life."

The heart in a human body has to be protected because

- the blood of life flows through the heart,
- the heart is the center of the body, and
- when the heart doesn't pump correctly the entire body is affected.

A Personal Heart Problem Story

When my nephew was born he had heart problems. He wasn't expected to survive past the first twenty-four hours, but thanks to my sister-in-law and her protective care, he was able to live a fairly normal life. When he was little, though, his lips would turn blue due to lack of oxygen and blood flow, but he was smart as a whip so apparently this did not affect his brain.

My nephew was a couple of years older than my son. When Brian was little we would pray for Jason all the time. My son would ask, "Mom, why can't God heal Jason?" And he would say, "Mom, we have to pray for Jason, for him to get better so he can run and play like me."

Year after year Brian would pray for Jason because my son had a heart condition too—he loved his cousin and his heart hurt when his cousin couldn't run and play like he did. When Jason had to have his first heart surgery at the Mayo Clinic the summer after he finished fifth grade, and when he underwent the second step of the surgery the summer following sixth grade, we prayed and prayed and waited on updates.

I think that my son is a doctor today because of his love and concern for his cousin Jason.

When Jason died right before his senior year of high school, my son was devastated. Jason's heart had been fixed the year before at Mayo Clinic, and for the first time in his life, he could ride a bike, drive a car, and shoot hoops. But for some reason, his heart just quit working one night. My son's heart was broken. He and Jason shared special cousin secrets and jokes, and as time passes, my son likes recalling some of the funnier times with his cousin.

We never know all the ways God is working in our kids' lives. We must continually keep them in the Lord's family, in the church, and in His Word, praying with them when problems arise and teaching them that when there is something bothering them, they should automatically go before the Lord. And we must also teach them that God doesn't always answer their prayers the way they want Him to. Sometimes we have to sit quietly before the Lord and listen for Him.

One Wise Single Mom's Personal Theology

A wise single mom once told me that she purposefully worked with her children on being quiet. I asked her what she meant, and she said, "There are times, like in a doctor's office or in the car, I tell my children they need to be quiet. I am teaching them to sit quietly without saying anything. How else will children understand Psalm 46:10, which says, 'Be still, and know that I am God,' and know that this verse applies to them?" Think on that important concept for a few minutes. Will your child know how to sit quietly before the Lord in order to hear God speaking to him or to her?

A Dad Teaches His Daughter to Listen to Her Heart

My friend Barry Cummings, a single dad in Florida, shared with me about how he used a crisis situation to help his daughter explore how her heart felt and how she could use those feelings to minister to others. His daughter was six years old at the time. Barry says,

On April 27, 2011, my hometown was devastated by an F-5 tornado, and many people lost everything. Nineteen lost their lives in Northwest Alabama that day. Help began to pour in soon after the weather was safe.

I became involved with a ministry that cooked and provided meals to the victims and recovery workers. Being a single dad and wanting to teach my six-year-old daughter, Tara, about serving God and serving people in need, I made the decision to start taking her with me to see service in action. It's my responsibility to help mold her heart to love God and have compassion for others, but what can a six-year-old do to help? The answer came from some blank paper and crayons.

We love to draw, so at night we would draw and color pictures of Jesus, crosses, etc., and the next day she would hand them out at the tables when the people were eating. One picture stood out, and the story she would tell melted their hearts along with mine.

The picture depicted a tornado with rainbow colors along with some crosses, angels, and pets. She called it the "Rainbow Tornado," but it was a good tornado that brought back the things people lost that day. People's homes, belongings, pets, and their hope. People got such a blessing from something so simple, along with hearing the Gospel shared.

People came from all over the U.S., and even some from other countries to help with the recovery efforts in Northwest Alabama. It amazed me to see how much joy people got out of Tara and me serving together. Many people came to Christ through that tragedy. That terrible day was seven years ago, and just like in her "Rainbow Tornado" picture, our town and area has been built back strong. This was a lesson of compassion and love for Tara and myself that we continue to use to this day.

Wow, what an example of a godly single parent. He could have moaned and groaned and said, "Why me?" but he didn't. He got busy and got involved in a local ministry. Then he took his daughter with him to that ministry. I imagine many people were blessed by little Tara. I also imagine that as Tara grows, she understands the deep love of the Father even more. She has been acquainted with trauma and watched as God's people ministered.

Deepening Our Relationship with Father God

The rest of our passage gives instructions that will help us deepen our relationship with God. These are also wise instructions to pass on to our children.

Proverbs 4:24 addresses being careful with our words: "Keep your mouth free of perversity; keep corrupt talk far from your lips" (NIV).

In our world today, it can be difficult for our kids to avoid careless banter, corrupt talk, lies, and gossip because it is so easy to do these things on social media. It is much easier to lie when the person is not standing right in front of you. It's easy to just type out a fast message and click send, or snap a snarky picture and send it out.

As parents we need to keep our eyes fixed on Jesus and not get tangled up in the world's lies. "Let your eyes look straight ahead; fix your gaze directly before you" (v. 25 NIV).

It is easy to begin to believe lies about what other people experience. We see our neighbor driving a new car and think, "If only I had a better job" or "If only I could win the lottery. Then my troubles would be over, and I would be driving that new car."

We see beautiful-looking people on the covers of magazines. We want to look like them, dress like them, and be wealthy like they are. We can begin pulling away from the life God has in store for us and from a deep relationship with Him.

Keep your feet on level ground. "Give careful thought to the paths for your feet and be steadfast in all your ways. Do not turn to the right or the left; keep your foot from evil" (vv. 26–27 NIV).

It is hard to walk and keep our balance when the ground we are walking on is crooked or filled with deep ravines or large boulders. Ever try standing upright when walking on a mountainous path that has huge boulders on it? Sometimes you have to grab onto a tree branch to keep from falling, or you have to put out your hands to climb over a rock in the middle of the path.

Keeping your feet on level ground might mean removing moral dilemmas that pull you away from God. Let's divide this up into two different categories. First are the moral dilemmas that affect our children:

- Lying about their activities
- Cheating on a test
- Doing something because everyone else is doing it (drugs, alcohol, etc.)
- Having any form of sex
- Using the Internet to find sexual sites or information
- Bullying others
- Dressing provocatively
- Disrespecting authority—in your home and outside your home

Second are the moral issues that affect you. I'm sure you can think of your own, but here are a few to get you started:

- Watching R-rated movies
- Reading inappropriate material
- Looking the other way at work when someone steals from the company
- Engaging in sex outside of marriage
- Stealing
- Viewing pornography

Think about ways to remove these temptations from your life. Did you know that pornography use is one of the main reasons many marriages fail, and that it is a growing problem among women as well as men? If you are a woman, you need to understand what porn does to a man so you'll be aware that any man who is into porn is not marriage material.

In his article "Has Your Porn Addiction Made You Absent?" Neill Morris writes that pornography makes "wives miss all the things that a loving husband can give, i.e., his attention, his affection, his honor, his affirmation, his loving touch, his listening ear, his romancing, his intimacy, his caring. When we are so preoccupied with ourselves, how could we possibly make her feel secure in our love? But in that scenario, we are so gripped by our love of porn and of self that we have nothing to give her."[3]

If you are a man, it would be prudent to read the rest of the article. Porn is an addiction, and it will eventually destroy you. Morris says, "I have talked with these men and counseled them, one-on-one, during the past fourteen years—more than four thousand men, each with his own story of destruction through the cancer of pornography and its seeming irresistible attraction."[4]

Your Single-Parent Family

Take time to figure out how you think these verses in Proverbs 4 apply to how you are raising your children. Study these verses. Discuss them with your children. There is a lot of wisdom that single parents can glean, and it is wisdom that can change the course of your single-parent family.

What Happened to Shelly and Her Kids?

Shelly went back to school and is now Dr. Shelly Melia, assistant professor of childhood education and program director for the master of arts degrees in children's ministry and family ministry at Dallas Baptist University. She serves as the associate dean for the Graduate School of Ministry and is a counselor specializing in grief and trauma in children.

Her kids are growing, and her older son is now finishing his first year in college. Her middle child, her daughter, is a high school senior this year, and her younger son is now fifteen and in high school. Life has been good, but not without the usual trauma and crisis all of us as single parents have experienced.

Last year her daughter was on a mission trip to Utah when Shelly got a call at eleven at night saying that Lexi was sick and had been taken to the local hospital. As Shelly drove herself to the airport at three in the morning to catch a flight, she thought, *Why do I have to do this alone?*

It was four days before she could bring her daughter home. Lexi had *E. coli.* Shelly brought her daughter home only to have to take her to the emergency room when Lexi's kidneys shut down and she had to be put on dialysis. It was quite a summer with Lexi in and out of the hospital several times. Mom had to face her daughter's surgery as a single mom alone. Lexi finally made it out of the crisis, but it was rough going for several weeks.

Like all single parents, Shelly did what she had to do. She put her life on hold in order to care for her daughter. She prayed and worried and handed her concerns over to Jesus.

The best way to influence our kids and turn them toward the Lord Jesus Christ is to model being a Christian and maintain a strong prayer life and a joy-filled faith walk.

"Let us fix our eyes on Jesus, the author and perfecter of our faith, who for the joy set before him endured the cross, scorning its shame, and sat down at the right hand of the throne of God" (Hebrews 12:2).

GOING DEEPER

1. How do we "engrave" God's words upon our hearts? Upon our children's hearts?

2. What have you discovered about your child's heart? What character weaknesses do you need to work on with your child?

3. How does comprehending that the heart is the center of our emotional being help you in understanding some of the hurts you have experienced in your life, such as a divorce or the death or desertion of a partner?

4. How can you help your child put away perversity from his or her mouth and not talk out of both sides of his or her mouth?

5. How will you help your child (and yourself) avoid the following offenses?

   • Careless banter
   • Lies
   • Gossip

6. What causes you to take your eyes off Christ?

7. Proverbs 4:26–27 instructs us, "Make level paths for your feet and take only ways that are firm. Do not swerve to the right or the left; keep your foot from evil." What do you think "Make level paths for your feet" means?

8. Considering everything in this chapter, what stands out as the most important thing you need to do with your children?

12

Serving Our Lord

Yes, Single Parents Are Worthy to Serve

It was late, and I was driving back to my home in Broken Arrow, Oklahoma, after being in meetings all day in Oklahoma City. I served on the Child Care Advisory Committee and was chairing the committee to rewrite the licensing regulations. That in itself was a pretty stressful situation; add in the two-hour drive back to Broken Arrow, and you can understand how tired I was. As my mind switched from child care licensing issues, it went to thinking about my friend Mandie.

Mandie was a single mom who had cancer. Her prognosis wasn't good. She had recently come to know Christ as her personal Savior and was enthusiastically soaking up God's Word. She was in treatment and, as far as I knew, had not been diagnosed as terminal.

For some reason, I felt a pressing urge to go by her house. Keep in mind that it was late, I was exhausted, and I hadn't seen my kids all day. But this urge was so great that I knew I had to run by her house. I knocked on the door, and her brother answered. He said, "Thank goodness you got the message. We've been trying to reach you all day. Mandie needs to talk to you right now. She wants you to plan her funeral."

What? Plan her funeral?

My first comment was, "I really think that is something the family will want to do," but the brother assured me they didn't even want to think about her dying, let alone plan her funeral. As Mandie entered the living room, her brother and sister excused themselves, not only walking out of the room, but out of the house. So there I was, alone with my friend who wanted to plan her funeral.

Mandie explained, "My family are not Christians, and I want a Christian funeral. I know I'm dying. I don't have much time left. I want you to help me pick out some Scriptures and some songs, and I want you to play the piano." Well, that was a tall order! I didn't think I was up to this assignment, but I quickly said a prayer and asked God to guide me in this huge request. Now here is the really cool part of the evening. The first thing she wanted to do was look at the Twenty-third Psalm.

> The Lord is my shepherd, I shall not want;
>   he makes me lie down in green pastures.
> He leads me beside still waters;
>   he restores my soul.
> He leads me in paths of righteousness
>   for his name's sake.
> Even though I walk through the valley of the shadow
>   of death,
>   I fear no evil;
> for thou art with me;
>   thy rod and thy staff,
>   they comfort me.
>
> Psalm 23:1–4 RSV

As we read through this psalm, the Lord allowed me to explain what it meant for her as she was dying. God was waiting for her.

In heaven He was going to refresh her soul, and there would be nothing to fear.

I also told her that it was a privilege to walk partway through the "valley of the shadow of death" with her, but at some point, she would have to leave me and continue with the Lord and maybe even an angel holding her hand, guiding her. A big smile crept across her face.

Her husband had left her when he found out she had cancer. She discovered later that he had been having an affair before the diagnosis. He was fighting her for custody of their four-year-old son. Her life had been so full of stress and fear, but now as she was dying and preparing to enter heaven, she could be assured that the Lord would take care of the things on earth, including her precious little boy.

When I got home late that night, I realized it was the Lord who gave me that urging to go by Mandie's house. I know God was in the planning of her Christian funeral. My teenage kids were already asleep, and after I checked on them, I stumbled into my room and fell into bed, full of joy on the inside that I was able to serve my friend and serve my God.

Worthy Enough to Serve

When I first became a single parent, I didn't feel worthy enough to serve. Oh, I knew God had my back, and I knew He was providing for me. But serve? That was a far-fetched idea. Then slowly, I began to notice how God was using me in various situations. Sometimes it was just as a listening ear. Other times it was helping a distraught single parent deal with an out-of-control kid. Then, in our Bible study class, people started asking me questions about my devotion time and my relationship with the Lord.

Little by little, I realized I was serving our God. It wasn't anything grandiose like teaching a Bible study class, but it was what I could do at the time. Just like in the story above with Mandie, it was a matter of paying attention to the pull on my heartstrings and being aware of someone else's situation.

In this chapter we are going to look at three different stories in Luke 21:1–4, 2 Kings 7:3–9, and Genesis 16:1–13. These are stories about people who were worthy enough to serve, but none would have been counted worthy enough to serve by the people of their day.

I want this chapter to be an encouragement to you to serve the Lord in whatever way you deem He is calling you. Let's explore how God can use every circumstance for His glory and how you are worthy enough to experience God's mercy and in turn give back to Him.

Keep in mind that God doesn't look at what the people around us think. God looks at our hearts because He is a merciful God, and God looks at the potential we have to serve Him.

The Widow's Offering

The widow in Luke 21:1–4 probably didn't feel like she was worthy enough to serve.

> As Jesus looked up, he saw the rich putting their gifts into the temple treasury. He also saw a poor widow put in two very small copper coins. "Truly I tell you," he said, "this poor widow has put in more than all the others. All these people gave their gifts out of their wealth; but she out of her poverty put in all she had to live on."
>
> Luke 21:1–4 NIV

Many of us have read this story before. You might have heard ministers preach on it and workshop leaders quote it, but have you ever really sat down and contemplated how this story can affect your life as a single mom or dad?

What do we know about the widow?

1. She went to the same temple where the rich people attended.

2. She was poor.

3. She put in two very small copper coins.

4. Jesus noticed her.

5. Jesus talked about her.

6. She put in all she had to live on, and more than any of the others.

Are there any parts of this story that sound like your own? Do you sometimes feel like you don't fit in someplace, like at church? I know I felt that way for many years. Because of my divorce and feelings of not being good enough, I could not take part in Communion; I didn't feel worthy to partake of this holy replication of the Lord's Last Supper. It was so emotional to me and real that Christ gave His life for my wretched and now divorced life. Because I would play the piano softly throughout Communion, no one noticed that I wasn't taking part. To this day, years later, taking part in Communion is very emotional for me.

I imagine this poor widow didn't feel like she fit in with the wealthy people at the temple treasury. She was different because she was poor. She probably dressed differently and even looked different—I imagine her clothes were tattered and her sandals worn. We don't know what the widow was thinking; we just know she went to the temple. We also know she had a relationship with God because she didn't give of her surplus; she gave her everything to Him.

God used a poor widow to be an example to the disciples. Jesus talked about this woman to others. Whoa! Can you imagine Jesus talking about you?

I have seen many single parents give of their talents, time, and resources to serve Him. These are people who make a difference in the kingdom. Like this widow, most are not aware of how their lives are impacting other people.

Today, ministers and church leaders use the story of the poor widow to teach others that this widow was worthy enough to serve.

Not only are single parents worthy enough to serve, but children raised in single-parent homes can also serve. I have a friend who had quite the childhood. By all accounts she should not want to serve our Lord, but Kay Farmer is serving in a mighty way. Like the widow in Luke, Kay is giving her all. She is a missionary overseas. She had to leave her invalid father here in the States and depend upon others to care for him.

Kay's Story

Everything I have ever done in my life, including as a child, has prepared me for what God called me to do. Nothing, absolutely nothing, was in vain. The good, the bad, and the ugly. All was to prepare me.

My parents divorced when I was five years old. We (my sister and I) lived with my dad, and he was a single parent. He did his best, but when I was ten, false accusations were made and we were removed from our home. My church leadership walked with us through this situation, and my Daddy fought hard and did whatever was required to get us back.

Before my dad got us back, we lived in two foster homes and then in a children's home for one year. Church leadership made sure we stayed in the same church through living in foster care and the children's home.

Because of our church family, JESUS was our constant in the middle of the chaos. It is for that reason I am where I am today. I understand that kids will face things out of their control, but as long as they know who to run to in the chaos, they can be saved from what statistics says is their reality. It's the reason why this Saturday I will be visiting a children's home here in Budapest, and I will be able to relate to every child there.

God uses it all for His glory!

185

Kay serves as the children's ministry leader where she is overseas this year. She has spent much of her own income to decorate and prepare a space for children. She reads Bible stories to children in local libraries. She is worthy enough to serve.

An Unlikely Group of People to Serve

An unlikely group of people who served in the Bible were four men with leprosy. Lepers were outcasts. They were literally made to live outside the city. Because leprosy was so contagious, other people didn't want them living within the walls of the city, and so these were people who did not fit in. And yet we read in 2 Kings how these people served others in their city.

> Now there were four men with leprosy at the entrance of the city gate. They said to each other, "Why stay here until we die? If we say, 'We'll go into the city'—the famine is there, and we will die. And if we stay here, we will die. So let's go over to the camp of the Arameans and surrender. If they spare us, we live; if they kill us, then we die."
> At dusk they got up and went to the camp of the Arameans. When they reached the edge of the camp, no one was there, for the Lord had caused the Arameans to hear the sound of chariots and horses and a great army, so that they said to one another, "Look, the king of Israel has hired the Hittite and Egyptian kings to attack us!" So they got up and fled in the dusk and abandoned their tents and their horses and donkeys. They left the camp as it was and ran for their lives.
> The men who had leprosy reached the edge of the camp, entered one of the tents and ate and drank. Then they took silver, gold and clothes, and went off and hid them. They returned and entered another tent and took some things from it and hid them also.
> Then they said to each other, "What we're doing is not right. This is a day of good news and we are keeping it to ourselves. If we wait until daylight, punishment will overtake us. Let's go at once and report this to the royal palace."
>
> 2 Kings 7:3–9 NIV

Visualize how destitute the lepers must have felt. There was a famine in their city, and the people were all hungry and waiting to die. There wasn't much hope for the people in the city or for the lepers, so we can imagine them saying, "Well, we can go where people won't accept us and wait to die, we can stay here by ourselves and wait to die, or we can go over to the enemy camp and hope for the best."

When they went into the vacant camp, the outcasts found a virtual paradise. They could eat all they wanted. They could take things, and no one would be the wiser. They could have hidden the plunder to keep for themselves.

What did the lepers do when they found the food and bounty?

1. Entered a tent and ate and drank
2. Took silver, gold, and clothes and hid them
3. Returned and entered another tent and took things and hid them
4. Felt guilty and decided to report what had happened
5. Shared with the very people who had mistreated them

They went at once to report to the royal palace what they had found. The outcasts didn't even wait until the next day. They opted to share this good news with others who hadn't treated them very well.

Have you ever felt you weren't treated well? Were you as forgiving as the lepers? Have you given back to those who didn't treat you well like the lepers did, and will you serve those people?

The Lord dispersed the Arameans, and then the Lord used the lepers to save everyone in their city. The lepers, even though they were outcasts, were worthy enough to serve.

Called to Serve Despite a Traumatic Early Life

If any of my friends and associates ever had an opportunity to consider herself an outcast and not worthy enough to serve, I think it would be Jennifer Maggio. Jennifer's story is amazing, and you can read about it in her book, *Overwhelmed: The Life of a Single Mom.* Her story starts when she was just a toddler and her mother was killed in a car accident. Her dad turned to alcohol and ended up marrying repeatedly during Jennifer's childhood and teen years. Jennifer was physically abused by stepmoms. She was sexually assaulted as a child by a stepfamily member. As a teen she fell in love with a boy who was abusive. Eventually, through a tumultuous relationship, she had two children with the abusive boyfriend. She raised those children alone and on public assistance.[1]

Jennifer was smart and knew the Lord Jesus Christ as her Savior. All through her childhood and teen years she had attended church faithfully while being physically abused at home, molested, dealing with a dad who was drunk most of the time, and stepmoms coming and going. She wanted more for herself and for her children. Her story is hers to tell, and I won't attempt to go into all the details. If you want to know more, read her compelling book.

What I do want you to know is that today Jennifer is CEO of the Life of a Single Mom. She is married and the mother of three children. She is serving the Lord and ministering to thousands of single moms. And that is not an exaggeration. I know because in 2015 she invited me to speak at her yearly single-mom conference. At that event there were one thousand moms in attendance. They came from all over the country just to spend the weekend with other single moms and to be fed the Word of God. Jennifer also helps churches set up single-mom groups.

Jennifer overcame all of the obstacles that Satan put in her way. She could have gone a different direction, but she held on to her faith. With the childhood she had, she has every right to be angry and bitter, but she isn't. Joy radiates from her, and God is using her vastly in His kingdom.

Perhaps you are saying, "Well, that's great for Jennifer. But I don't have the income to branch out like that." Or "I don't have the energy." Or "I have too many children." Or, or, or—you can have a dozen excuses, but God can overcome any excuse if you allow Him. Imagine being a slave and being told you have to have a baby, then imagine being cast out and sent on your way to fend for yourself and your child. This is what happened to one single mom in the Bible.

A Slave Serves Also

In chapter 4, "Supporting Your Children When You Have Them Part Time," we read about a woman named Hagar, but we concentrated on Abram's role. In this chapter Hagar's story is important.

Like many single parents today, Hagar lived through quite a struggle. Her life was all about serving her mistress, and through no fault of her own she was cast out of the home where she had lived for many years. She and her son must have felt like exiles as they were sent away. Let's read about this first single parent in the Bible. I'd venture to say few of us have had as tough a journey as this single mom.

> Now Sarai, Abram's wife, had borne him no children. But she had an Egyptian slave named Hagar; so she said to Abram, "The Lord has kept me from having children. Go, sleep with my slave; perhaps I can build a family through her."
>
> Abram agreed to what Sarai said. So after Abram had been living in Canaan ten years, Sarai his wife took her Egyptian slave Hagar and gave her to her husband to be his wife. He slept with Hagar, and she conceived.
>
> When she knew she was pregnant, she began to despise her mistress. Then Sarai said to Abram, "You are responsible for the wrong I am suffering. I put my slave in your arms, and now that she knows she is pregnant, she despises me. May the Lord judge between you and me."
>
> "Your slave is in your hands," Abram said. "Do with her whatever you think best." Then Sarai mistreated Hagar; so she fled from her.

The angel of the Lord found Hagar near a spring in the desert; it was the spring that is beside the road to Shur. And he said, "Hagar, slave of Sarai, where have you come from, and where are you going?"

"I'm running away from my mistress Sarai," she answered.

Then the angel of the Lord told her, "Go back to your mistress and submit to her." The angel added, "I will increase your descendants so much that they will be too numerous to count."

The angel of the Lord also said to her:

> "You are now pregnant
>   and you will give birth to a son.
> You shall name him Ishmael,
>   for the Lord has heard of your misery.
> He will be a wild donkey of a man;
>   his hand will be against everyone
>   and everyone's hand against him,
> and he will live in hostility
>   toward all his brothers."

She gave this name to the Lord who spoke to her: "You are the God who sees me," for she said, "I have now seen the One who sees me."

Genesis 16:1–13 NIV

What do we know about Hagar?

1. She was a slave.
2. She was given to her mistress's husband for him to impregnate.
3. She was mistreated by her mistress.
4. She ran away.
5. The Lord heard her cries and told her to go back and submit to Sarai.
6. He made a promise to her to increase her descendants so much that they would be too numerous to count.

7. The Lord told her what to name her child.
8. The Lord told her what her child was going to be like.
9. She told God that He was the God who saw her.

What Hagar realized was the truth. "You are the God who sees me" (v. 13). Do you realize that it is God who sees you, and it is God you must see? And God you must serve?

God's love for us is what makes us worthy enough to serve in His kingdom. Christ's sacrifice on the cross is what makes us worthy enough to serve in the family of God.

Like He has used the story of the widow and the story of the lepers, God has used the story of Hagar and Ishmael to further His kingdom. After realizing Hagar was loved and used by God, I connected with her story. We were both single parents, albeit her journey was much tougher than mine.

Hagar, the slave, was worthy enough to serve. Are you worthy enough to serve?

Single Parents Who Serve

The following are some stories of people who were worthy enough to serve even if they didn't always feel like they could.

David was a single dad whose teenage kids only visited every so often. He loved to fix things around the house, so he became the handyman for many single moms in his church.

Kelly was a single mom for years and now lived alone. She was also an older lady who didn't have a lot of money because an injury left her unable to work. Kelly had a servant's heart. A single mom in her group had made the comment that she wished she had more time to make a homemade meal for her son. Kelly, who was in severe pain most of the time, took her limited resources, her talent for cooking, and her time to prepare a homemade meal for this single mom who served in the military.

When Jack went through a divorce he allowed God to heal him, and then he became a divorce recovery expert, and he has helped hundreds of people in his area through his encouraging words and through single-parent and children's picnics. He knows how to advertise, and he uses this talent to promote single-parent family events in his church. His life has impacted hundreds of people in his community.

One older gentleman loved to work in his garage fixing things. He took this interest and started looking for old bicycles to rebuild. He now furnishes needy families with bicycles at Christmas. Through his talent and his time, he is meeting a need for parents who can't afford to purchase bikes for their children.

Ann always lacked self-confidence, but she was a good cook. She always had the ingredients in her home to make a fantastic meal. She made meals for shut-ins and for single-parent families who needed to know they mattered to someone at church.

Stacey's ex-husband is in jail and has been for several years. She went back to school and is now a registered nurse, and she ministers to the teens at church. They love her, and she mentors them through many trials.

How can you take your talents, hobbies, interests, and things you like to do, pair them up with your experiences, and use them for service to God?

God never wastes any experiences of those who love Him. He can use your story and your troubles to further His kingdom.

My Story

After I had been divorced and had raised my kids, I remarried, and my husband died of cancer in 1997. I thought my life was over. I was just going to sit in a rocking chair and live out my final days. Oh boy, was I ever wrong. Five years later in 2002, I got a call from Steve Grissom, the developer of DivorceCare.[2] He wanted to know if I'd like to write DivorceCare for Kids, DC4K.[3]

My life had moved on. I was busy working at my child care center, serving on some state committees, and speaking at a lot of churches about single-parent ministries. I had just remarried two weeks before Steve called me. Steve told me to think about it and said that in a couple of months he was going to call me for an answer.

I prayed and prayed.

I visited with my ailing mother. She said, "Go where the Lord leads you."

I talked to my grown-up kids. They said, "Mom, we are grown-up now with lives of our own. Go. Write the program."

I talked to my child care staff. One of my long-term teachers said, with tears streaming down her face, "Linda, go. Why do you think we have worked so hard all these years? It was so God would get you out in a bigger realm where more children could be impacted."

The night before Steve was to call I told the Lord I still wasn't sure what to do. Taking that position meant moving from Oklahoma to North Carolina. When I asked my new husband, Bruce, what to do he said, "I so much believe in what God has in store for you to do with children that I will quit my job and follow you wherever the Lord takes you. I know He will provide a job for me."

I must be a slow learner because when I went to bed that night I was still confused. I wanted to make sure the Lord was in this, and I wanted confirmation. Finally, I dozed off to sleep. In the middle of the night I woke to loud music playing. We lived out in the country. We had a huge field behind our house. I got up and all was silent. I went downstairs and looked around. Nothing, no noise. I opened the patio door and listened outside. Nothing. So I went back to bed.

Just as I closed my eyes the music started again. This time I recognized the song. It was "Wherever He Leads I'll Go" by Baylus Benjamin McKinney. *Okay, God.* I got my answer. I knew beyond a shadow of a doubt that God was in this new adventure. Going from being a broken single mom wondering if I was going to survive to being offered an opportunity that would impact thousands of little kids' lives was indeed a God thing. God was in charge. God provided and He continues to provide.

Today DC4K is in many places around the world. There are more than 4,000 churches worldwide equipped with the DC4K program. There have been 128,000 kids whose lives have been changed, children who have been equipped with the *DC4K Activity Book*. Who knew this divorced lady from a little town called Broken Arrow in Oklahoma running a small child care center would be used of God for such a mighty purpose? God knew and God provided.

Remember, God never wastes any experiences for those who love Him. He can use your story and your troubles to further His kingdom.

What about Mandie?

No one in Mandie's family realized she was dying. Just a few weeks after planning her funeral, she went to the hospital for the last time. She wanted me to be there as much as possible. Every time I went, she would ask me to sing the praise songs we sang at church.

One night I got a call from the hospital. The nurse said, "Linda, would it be possible for you to come up and sing those praise songs to Mandie? When you sing to her, her blood pressure goes down and she becomes so calm and peaceful. Some of her family are here, and even though she has lapsed into a coma, she is very agitated."

I was tired and really in no mood to drive half an hour to the hospital, but I knew this was the Lord calling. When I walked into her room and saw what her family was doing, I turned right around and went to the nurses' station. I said, "If you want me to help out tonight, you'll need to ask her family to leave. Do you know that they are prying open her eyes and showing her pictures of her son and saying, 'Look, Mandie, it's your little boy. He needs you. You have to live to care for him'? Her sister is combing her hair and putting makeup on her."

Her family could not accept the fact that she was dying. They couldn't accept the fact that Mandie was ready. They couldn't accept that Mandie was already on her way home. I believe she was seeing into heaven, and her family was irritating her by trying to force her to stay here on earth.

The nurses asked the family to leave. I climbed into bed next to Mandie, and I sang my heart out. Tears streamed down her face. Tears streamed down my face. She calmed down. I left late that night, and I knew I'd never see her again—she was on her way to heaven. That was late Saturday night, and Mandie left this earth on Monday morning.

As I stated before, God never wastes an experience. Before I helped Mandie on her journey heavenward, I helped a single dad in the last two weeks of his life. I'm the one who told him he was dying and that it was okay to leave this place. When my own husband had cancer and was dying, the chaplain at the VA hospital asked me, "Have you ever been with someone who was dying?" When I told him yes, he said, "That was your training ground. This will be harder because he is your husband."

He was right, but because of past experiences, I was able to minister to my husband's family while he was dying. I was able to minister to my husband as he was seeing into heaven. Serving God throughout trials creates an intimate relationship with the Father.

What will you do with the experiences, trials, tribulations, and hurt you have had brought upon you? I hope you will feel worthy enough to serve because when you serve and comfort the hurting, you are doing it for kingdom causes.

Praise be to the God and Father of our Lord Jesus Christ, the Father of compassion and the God of all comfort, who comforts us in all our troubles, so that we can comfort those in any trouble with the comfort we ourselves receive from God. For just as we share abundantly in the sufferings of Christ, so also our comfort abounds through Christ. If we are distressed, it is for your comfort and salvation; if we are comforted, it is for your comfort, which produces in you patient endurance of the same sufferings we suffer. And our hope for you is firm, because we know that just as you share in our sufferings, so also you share in our comfort.

2 Corinthians 1:3–7 NIV

GOING DEEPER

1. In the story of the poor widow in Luke 21:1–4, the Scripture says she put in more than all of the others. What do you think this means?

2. What are some reasons that single parents feel they don't fit in at church?

3. What are your thoughts about the story in 2 Kings 7:3–9 about the lepers? Can you serve a community of people who haven't treated you well?

4. How about a church group that hasn't treated you well as a single parent? Can you serve with them or serve them?

5. Is it possible for you to serve the people in your church in some way?

6. What are your talents, your hobbies, and things you like to do?

7. How can these talents and hobbies be used for the family of God?

8. What are some experiences you have been through that the Lord can use to help others who might be experiencing the same type of situation?

Conclusion

"The Lord Will Guide You"

I hope this book has encouraged you to discover the richness of a faith walk. I also want this book and the stories in it to provide hope and help as you raise your kids. I hope you will find answers to life problems and raising a family in the Scriptures.

It's important for single parents to discover the depth of a prayerful life and pass that on to their children by modeling it and taking everything to our Father. Even today my kids know they can call me about a friend or a problem and I will lift them and that situation up to our Lord.

I hope by now you know you are not alone in your journey of parenting kids in a single-parent family.

There is so much I wanted to include, and I keep thinking of passages of Scripture and stories to tell. But each of you can find your own passages that mean something to you and to your particular situation. And each of you will have your own stories to tell and share with other single parents.

One More Thing

If you feel your child or children are out of control, step back, regroup, and reorganize. Then go to your children and tell them you have let things get out of control. Apologize to them. Do this at a calm time when everyone is happy. Have a family meeting where you bring in pizza or serve something special, or go to a local restaurant. Make it a festive occasion. Explain that you are going to be giving them control over their own lives and you'll do that through a lot of choices. Explain they will have responsibilities. Set up a few boundaries and explain in advance what they are. Have each kid sign an agreement so you know they understand. The main thing is to be the adult in the home.

And finally, keep on keeping on, my friends!

May abundant blessings be yours as you grow and mature in the Lord.

"The Lord will guide you continually, giving you water when you are dry and restoring your strength. You will be like a well-watered garden, like an ever-flowing spring" (Isaiah 58:11 NLT).

Notes

Introduction: Life Lessons Single Parents Can Learn from the Bible

1. See www.dc4k.org.
2. See https://blog.dc4k.org.
3. *Single Parents: Is Your Church Meeting Their Unique Needs?* (Wake Forest, NC: Church Initiative, Inc., 2017). See https://www.careleader.org/ebooks-single-parents/.
4. *Attract Families to Your Church and Keep Them Coming Back* (Nashville: Abingdon Press, 2014).

Chapter 1: Loneliness: One of the Hardest Parts of Being a Single Parent

1. David and Teresa Ferguson and Bruce and Joyce Walker, *Discovering Intimacy: Relating to God and Others as Single Adults* (Austin, Texas: Intimacy Press, 2000), 5.
2. Carmen Hoffman, *Single Parent Magazine*, August 1998.
3. Single & Parenting is a thirteen-week Christ-centered and video-based program for single parents. See http://www.singleandparenting.org.
4. Hoffman, *Single Parent Magazine*.

Chapter 2: Developing a Healthy Single-Parent Family

1. Mike Klumpp, *The Single Dad's Survival Guide: How to Succeed as a One-Man Parenting Team* (Colorado Springs: WaterBrook Press, 2003), 56.
2. Certain details of this story have been changed to protect the identities of those involved.
3. DivorceCare is a thirteen-week faith-based program for those who have gone through or who are experiencing a divorce. It is hosted by local churches. See www.divorcecare.org.
4. GriefShare is a thirteen-week faith-based program to help people grieving the death of a loved one. See www.griefshare.org.

5. Robert Beeson, *Going Solo: Hope and Healing for the Single Mom or Dad* (Carol Stream, IL: Tyndale House, 2018), 93–94.

6. Tim Elmore, "The Research on What Creates Satisfied and Successful Kids," *Growing Leaders*, March 7, 2018, https://growingleaders.com/blog/research-creates-satisfied-successful-kids/.

7. See https://news.harvard.edu/gazette/story/2017/04/over-nearly-80-years-harvard-study-has-been-showing-how-to-live-a-healthy-and-happy-life/.

8. List adapted from Linda Ranson Jacobs, "Ten Tips to Create an Every-Other-Weekend Home for the Child of Divorce," *Kids & Divorce* (blog), July 13, 2018, https://blog.dc4k.org/archives/6610.

Chapter 3: Behavior and Discipline Issues

1. Charles Allen, *God's Psychiatry: Healing for Your Troubled Heart* (Grand Rapids, MI: Revell, 2015), 35.

2. *Merriam-Webster Unabridged*, s.v. "discipline," http://unabridged.merriam-webster.com/unabridged/discipline.

3. Jane Nelsen, Cheryl Erwin, and Carol Delzer, *Positive Discipline for Single Parents: A Practical Guide to Raising Children Who Are Responsible, Respectful, and Resourceful* (Rocklin, CA: Prima Publishing, 1994), 6.

4. Dr. Henry Cloud and Dr. John Townsend, *Boundaries with Kids* (Grand Rapids, MI: Zondervan, 1998), 16–17.

Chapter 4: Supporting Your Children When You Have Them Part Time

1. The name and some of the details have been altered at the request of the person who shared this story.

2. DivorceCare is a thirteen-week support group for people experiencing a separation or divorce. See www.divorcecare.org.

3. Most of the material in this "Parental Conflict" section was originally published in a blog post by Linda Ranson Jacobs, "The Big Overwhelming Variable That Causes Kids of Divorce Anxiety," *Kids & Divorce* (blog), April 19, 2018, https://blog.dc4k.org/archives/6322.

4. "Statistics," the Fatherless Generation, accessed February 10, 2018, https://thefatherlessgeneration.wordpress.com/statistics/.

5. Kathy Rodriguez, *Healing the Father Wound* (Enumclaw, WA: Pleasant Word, 2008), x–xi.

Chapter 5: Learning to Accept Other People into Your Child's Life

1. We are not talking about things that would hurt a child such as abuse, neglect, or sexual molestation. If you suspect any of these things, you need to call child protective services in your state.

2. Joshua A. Krisch, "The Science of Dad and the 'Father Effect,'" *Fatherly*, December 27, 2018, https://www.fatherly.com/health-science/science-benefits-of-fatherhood-dads-father-effect/.

3. Gail Gross, "The Important Role of Dad," *Life* (blog), *HuffPost*, June 12, 2014, https://www.huffpost.com/entry/the-important-role-of-dad_b_5489093.

Chapter 6: Living Faith in Desperate Times

1. Some of the material in this "Stressful Lives" section was previously published in a blog post by Linda Ranson Jacobs, "Stress and the Brain in Children of Divorce," *DivorceMinistry4Kids* (blog), February 10, 2012, http://divorceministry 4kids.com/2012/stress-and-the-brain-in-children-of-divorce/.

2. Some of the material in this "What Living under Constant Stress Does to Us" section was previously published in a blog post by Linda Ranson Jacobs, "Stress-busting Tips for Kids in Divorce," *Kids & Divorce* (blog), May 15, 2017, https://blog.dc4k.org/archives/2426.

3. Charles Stone, "How Going to Church Benefits Brain and Body," *Charles-Stone.com*, September 10, 2015, http://charlesstone.com/how-going-to-church -benefits-brain-and-body/.

4. Stone, "Church Benefits Brain and Body."

Chapter 7: Reaching Out and Being Vulnerable

1. Details have been changed in order to protect this family.

2. From the reference notes for 1 Kings 20:35 in the NIV Study Bible, Zondervan Corporation, 1985.

3. Sandra Aldrich, *From One Single Mother to Another* (Ventura, CA: Regal Books, 1991), 133.

4. Russell Moore, "Parenting and Work: Helping Our Children Gain a Sense of Belonging," *The Ethics & Religious Liberty Commission of the Southern Baptist Convention*, May 23, 2018, http://erlc.com/resource-library/articles/ parenting-and-work-helping-our-children-gain-a-sense-of-belonging.

5. For more ideas on kids helping around the home, see the article "Single Parent: Free Help with Household Chores!" by Linda Ranson Jacobs at https:// blog.dc4k.org/archives/3936.

6. Aldrich, *From One Single Mother to Another*, 133.

Chapter 8: Glorifying God in Single-Parent Life

1. See https://www.facebook.com/TheWidowsPeek/.

Chapter 9: How to Cope with Irritations

1. From the text note for Exodus 10:19 in the NIV Study Bible, Zondervan Corporation, 1985.

Chapter 10: Learning to Depend on God's Timing

1. D. G. Sciortino, "There's Scientific Evidence That Clutter Causes Anxiety," *Hampton Bay Medical News*, February 14, 2018, http://hamptonbaymedicalnews. com/2018/02/14/theres-scientific-evidence-that-clutter-causes-anxiety/.

2. Sherrie Bourg Carter, PsyD, "Why Mess Causes Stress: 8 Reasons, 8 Remedies," *Psychology Today*, March 14, 2012, https://www.psychologytoday.com/us /blog/high-octane-women/201203/why-mess-causes-stress-8-reasons-8-remedies.

3. Erin Doland, "Scientists Find Physical Clutter Negatively Affects Your Ability to Focus, Process Information," *unclutterer*, March 29, 2011, https://unclutterer.com/2011/03/29/scientists-find-physical-clutter-negatively-affects-your-ability-to-focus-process-information/.

4. See https://pdxscholar.library.pdx.edu/cgi/viewcontent.cgi?article=1050&context=socwork_fac.

Chapter 11: Modeling Biblical Principles for Children

1. Fred Rogers, *The World According to Mister Rogers* (New York: Hyperion, 2003), 187.

2. Biblical Parenting Thought Exchange email, August 9, 2013. You can sign up for these emails at http://www.biblicalparenting.org/parentingtips.asp.

3. Neill Morris, "Has Your Porn Addiction Made You Absent?" *CovenantEyes*, December 14, 2016, http://www.covenanteyes.com/2016/12/14/has-your-addiction-made-you-absent/.

4. Morris, "Has Your Porn Addiction Made You Absent?"

Chapter 12: Serving Our Lord

1. Jennifer Maggio, *Overwhelmed: The Life of a Single Mom* (Baton Rouge, LA: TLSM Publishing, 2017). See also https://thelifeofasinglemom.com/.

2. www.divorecare.org

3. www.dc4k.org

Linda Ranson Jacobs is the senior writer and content developer for DC4K. She has written numerous articles for pastors and children's pastors about caring for single-parent families and about how to provide nuanced care to children who have behavioral issues and have faced life traumas, such as fractured families and the deaths of family members. She contributes to many podcasts, blogs, and periodicals, including *Kids & Divorce*, (blog.dc4k.org), Hope4 HurtingKids.com, BiblicalParenting.org, *Chained No More* radio show, *Children's Ministry Magazine*, and *KidzMatter Magazine*.

Linda is a pioneering leader in the areas of children and divorce and of single-parent families' needs. Both divorced and widowed, as a single mom Linda learned firsthand the emotional and support needs of broken families and developed a passion to help hurting families. As a children's ministry director, children's program developer, speaker, author, trainer, and therapeutic child care center owner, Linda has assisted countless single-parent families.

In 2004, Linda created and developed the DivorceCare for Kids (DC4K) program, a ministry tool designed to bring healing, comfort, and coping and communication skills to the children of divorce. For eight years, she served as Church Initiative's DC4K executive director and is now the Church Initiative ambassador and serves on the editorial team with Church Initiative. She spreads the word about DC4K and teaches ministry leaders how to create a family-friendly church for single parents and their children, as well as how to help kids who have challenging behaviors.

Made in the USA
Middletown, DE
07 December 2022

17352859R00116